HACK PROOF YOUR BUSINESS

Featuring 12 IT Experts Nationwide

Prominence Publishing
www.prominencepublishing.com

Hack Proof Your Business/Chris Wiser. -- 1st ed.
ISBN 978-1-988925-43-1

Contents

Foreword

By Chris Wiser

Cybersecurity is one of the most critical issues of today's business environment.

As a former IT services firm owner, I know how critical it is to have a business threat mitigation plan in place, and what is even more important – how critical it is to have an expert you can turn to when things need to be planned out and recovered.

More than likely you are a business owner reading this right now, and it is ABSOLUTELY critical that you take IT seriously. Budget, plan and execute.

Your entire business runs on technology. What would happen if every piece of technology in your business was just shut down or you were locked out of it?

That is exactly what 'Hack Proof Your Business' is all about. A collection of IT & Cybersecurity experts that have come together to give you an outline on what to do in order to protect your business and your livelihood from cybersecurity threats. We talk about 'Hack Proofing' your business, but in reality, there is no way to actually do this in the long term other than best practices and preparation for a CONTROLLED recovery.

One thing I will tell you is that NO BUSINESS is too small to avoid this, and you need to prepare.

- Hire a Cybersecurity Expert.

- Make a budget.

- DO NOT BE CHEAP and think 'hacking will never happen to me', because it will happen to everyone.

Enjoy the book and watch for future editions!

Chris Wiser

CEO – The Wiser Agency

Speaker / Trainer / Entrepreneur Coach

Real Life Hacking

By Umut Bitlisli

In 2001, I found myself in New York City, just days after the September 11th attack. In fact, I was there on September 21st to sign a contract for a four-month stint doing tech work in the city. My thinking was, NYC needs to be rebuilt, and I took the opportunity to drive cross-country in my 1992 Honda Accord, back to my home of the east coast. Not too long after the move, William Alpert and I drove around Battery Park—he drove while I rode shotgun with a 15 dbi Yagi antenna in my hand picking up Wi-Fi networks, using Netstumbler to document all these open wireless networks: back then, security was always an afterthought. When Wi-Fi first came out, vendors were more interested in making it easy to use and adopt than making it safe. It's usually the case with any technology, we're first just really impressed that we've accomplished something. I mean, how cool was it that you could take a laptop into the bathroom and surf the internet?

I've been in the computing field since 1992, so I've had my fair share of setting up security systems. My first firewall appliance was in 1999 for the now-defunct San Francisco Bay Guardian Newspaper. I was one of three guys in the IT department and before we got our hands on it, the system had an open relay which let spammers through. The Guardian had approximately 150 users and their Act 4.0 server would crash daily; we'd always be called on to re-index it. After working at the Guardian, I moved to Silicon Valley for work.

Today, in 2019, cyber-security is still constantly in threat. It feels like you hear about a new breach all the time. Here are three real-life hacking examples and my "Hack-Proof" tips for each situation.

Case Study #1: Russians Hacking Your Server

July 25th 1999, Poway, California

Jeff Adzima and Aaron Lewis

It was a paltry 95-degree morning when Jeff Adzima, owner of a small ISP (Internet Service Provider) and his associate Aaron Lewis walked into their office. Jeff had received a phone call from one of his web server business clients saying his website wasn't working.

Jeff walked into the server room and immediately noticed some red Cyrillic letters on the screen:

Вы были взломаны!

(You've been Hacked!)

Jeff hollered to Aaron, "There's this writing on the server! It looks Russian."

"UNPLUG IT FROM THE INTERNET!" Aaron hollered back. Jeff unplugged the server from its T1 connection.

"Crap, what happened?" asked Jeff. Aaron and Jeff immediately started digging through their configurations. Both their hearts sank. The server had been hacked. Luckily, they had backups, but since the IP address was known by the cyber criminals, Jeff and Aaron spent three weekends cleaning up the mess. Websites would not go back up until they could clean up the server, which happened repeatedly because it kept on getting re-infected. During the process, they had to order a DSL line as a stopgap for clients while the pair worked on hardening security on the T1 line. Client websites would have to run slow on the DSL line until the mess was cleaned up, but it was the best they could do under the circumstances; the T1 lines would take months to install.

It was because of this situation that Jeff started educating himself on firewalls and security. In turn, this led him to a future in Computer Security. As for Aaron, today he is Senior Engineer at Crowdstrike. Their website is a familiar red and white, with a bold tagline of "Breaches Stop Here."

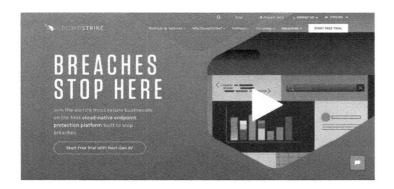

Hack-Proof Tips:

Connecting any computer to the internet without a firewall usually leads to an attack. A hardware appliance UTM (Unified Threat Management) should be configured to protect your server. Any outside access should be protected with 2FA (2 Factor-Authentication) and a VPN (Virtual Private Network). In addition, a SIEM (Security Information Event and Management) can be configured to log all incoming and outgoing connections. SIEMS are usually accompanied by a 24/7 SOC (Security Operations Center) who will monitor connections, contacting you if a security issue is detected.

Automated backups will ensure that servers can get back to work. These business continuity systems give you the advantage of replicating the role of a server. If a server goes down, it virtualizes the server, running it off its own hardware until the server is either repaired or replaced.

Case Study #2:

Marijuana Blackout – IoT Hacking

Armando Perez

Armando Perez builds Video Security Surveillance Systems. It was 2016 and Armando, owner of two companies, Hoosier Security and CCTV Dynamics, first encountered an IoT (Internet of Things) attack. IoT refers to any physical device that uses an IP address to connect through a network, usually to the internet. These include Wi-Fi enabled thermostats, speakers and cameras.

"There are basically three major companies that make recorders," explains Armando. "The biggest of them is Hikvision, who is not only owned but also operated by the Chinese government. Dahua, another of the three, is often rebadged as other brands. When you go to the store and purchase a unit, especially a cheap one, it's usually a Dahua. The issue with all of these Dahuas is that they have many security flaws, some possibly intentional."

Marijuana farms account for a surplus of growth in surveillance and security systems on the West coast, especially in Washington State. According to Armando, more than 50% of his business is from marijuana growing operations. He explains that these farms are all cash-strapped, that they generally need to invest their own funds into their operations and, as such, tend to go with lower-end security equipment.

It was these systems that were victims of the 2016 Mirai Botnet attack. During that time, IoT devices—such as camera systems recorders—were vulnerable. The Mirai botnet was able to take over these devices.

Initially, clients started calling Armando and mentioning that their cameras were renamed from "camera1" to "Hacked." While this initially seemed trivial, Armando explains how the hacks got worse. Cyber criminals started changing parameters in the units, like recording times, or they would turn the brightness all the way down so no picture would show. While seemingly just an annoyance, this threat led to a greater problem.

To remain in compliance with the rules of the governing Liquor Control Board, surveillance on marijuana operations must record for 45 days non-stop. If an audit was conducted of the two dozen farms using Armando's equipment, a farm could be fined, and if a repeat offender, have their license revoked. Perez states that luckily, none were fined. In most cases, he replaced the equipment because firmware updates were not available to upgrade the units and patch the security flaws. In cases where the units needed maintenance, he created VPNs (Virtual Private Networks) to contain the flaw.

It is interesting to note that the National Defense Authorization Act (NDAA) bans US government agencies from purchasing cameras and camera systems from Hikvision and Dahua, but they are not banned from usage in private businesses.

Hack-Proof Tips:

Botnets like Mirai will attack IOT devices that have built-in vulnerabilities. Sometimes, these devices cannot be patched against vulnerabilities, either due to manufacturer unwillingness, or because the option was never there in the first place. In these cases, replacing equipment is the best option. Another option is to put vulnerable IoT units onto a VPN, segregating network access via VLAN and adding 2FA to those connections.

Case Study #3:

Business Email Compromise

Harvey Gilbert

It was a hot day in July 2019. Ruth was sweating, but the air conditioning wasn't the issue. A phone call had just come into the Morristown, New Jersey law office where she worked. It was coming from client that sounded a little annoyed, "Ruth, why is Harvey asking for the $25,000 now? Didn't he just say yesterday that it would be in a couple of weeks?"

Harvey Gilbert, of Law Offices of Harvey Gilbert, had indeed said they would need the money for closing in about a week or two. However, the client explained that he had received an email from Harvey stating that the office needed the money *that day*. The puzzling thing was, Harvey didn't send any such email, so the client forwarded the email received to Ruth and it did indeed say it was from Harvey.

Harvey, we have a problem.

Upon inspection of the email, the following was evident: The telephone and fax numbers looked alike but were incorrect by one digit. The email requested a sum of $25,544 be wired to a particular account, with a note that, "Unfortunately, we are having trouble with our phones right now." The email was also sent to bogus versions of everyone involved in the legitimate transaction, including the title company, the bank and the attorney. The only real email was that of the client.

Harvey had been to a number of title agency seminars that preached the same thing: Fraud, fraud, fraud! Luckily, Harvey had implemented a confirmation policy that required verbal communication on both ends, before and after a transaction. In his 40+ years in law, Harvey had never experienced a single count of fraud, until now.

At the time of this writing, this crime is still being investigated by the Morristown Police Department. No money was ever lost by the client, but the hacker had apparently been monitoring his email and was waiting for his opportunity. This type of attack is called a Business Email Compromise.

According to the FBI, 2.7 billion dollars was lost to this type of hack in 2018 alone. In their annual Internet Crime Report, the Internet Crime Complaint Center (IC3) states that they've received 351,936 complaints, an average of more than 900 every day.

Hack-Proof Tips:

Email addresses are typically hacked via stolen passwords. Perform a dark web search for the email addresses in your company; if any credentials are found, immediately change the affected passwords and enable 2 Factor Authentication. Use a password manager. This will help generate and organize passwords and determine if password reuse is happening. A password manager will also show you how old passwords are and recommend renewals.

Get Your Hack-Proof On

Cyber criminals will attack. There's nothing we can do to prevent their attempts, but compromises don't need to happen. Minimize downtime and ransoms with proactive planning and hardening of your cybersecurity. Your best protection is a combination of Perimeter Security (UTM), Password Management and 2FA coupled with automated backup, and NextGen Endpoint Protection. Get your Hack-Proof on and work more confidently.

About the Author

Umut Bitlisli, founder of All Computers Go! In Chester, NJ, started his love affair with computers at the age of 13. He worked 30 different jobs before starting his current company. An immigrant, Umut emigrated from Turkey to the United States at the age of 4.

In 2003 he was recognized in Barron's Newspaper, Computer World and Channel 12 for his work in Wireless Security Auditing and he sold tools to various organizations including the Department of Defense, Sandia Weapons Lab and the Secret Service.

Bitlisli is a moderator of the Facebook group: IT & MSP Business Owner's Group with over 6000 Managed Service Providers worldwide. Bitlisli currently lives and works in Chester, NJ. When he's not working on his business, he enjoys time challenging others on the dance floor, being a foodie and watching movies on his apple tv.

Website: allcomputersgo.com
Phone: 908.879.1836
Umut@allcomputersgo.com

For a list of free resources, go to
www.allcomputersgo.com/free-resources

Employee Hygiene: Training Your Employees to Avoid Cyber Attacks

By Jeri Morgan

The changing landscape of how we communicate in business and how we manage our productivity is in constant flux. In my lifetime, I started working in a world before email, before widespread use of the Internet, before the fax machine, before cloud-based applications, and most certainly before Cyber Threats.

The thing I have always loved about being in the technology field is that the technology we use and the solutions we put into place for our clients are always moving at a high rate of speed. However, within the last few years the landscape has completely changed. The velocity at which Hackers and Cyber Criminals have been able to negatively impact – and in many cases shut businesses down permanently – is mind boggling.

What a typical business owner thinks a Cyber Attack is and what it actually is are completely different things. The business owner is picturing a brute force attack and most times they are envisioning a business much larger than their own as being at risk.

A Tale of Two Businesses

Earlier this year we received a call from a Service based company not too far from Denver where our office is headquartered. When our office assistant answered, she knew it was not a typical call. There was most definitely a sense of urgency to it.

The business owner - we will call him Robert - had come in to work to discover a shocking turn of events. They had been expecting a large deposit to post to the business account, but it had not been received. It turns out that their Finance Manager had responded to an email a few weeks back that appeared to have been sent by Robert from a personal email account. The email indicated that Robert was working with their CPA and that the Finance Manager should email her username and password for the cloud-based program that they used to run their business. Thinking this request was from her boss, the Finance Manager obliged immediately.

Unfortunately, the email was not from Robert but instead was from a hacker who promptly changed the bank account details that credit card transactions would deposit to. This ended up being a $25,000 mistake. Authorities were notified and many months of investigation, clean up, and recovery were ahead of them.

You may find this story hard to believe but the truth is we hear similar stories every day. Similarly, the next story may be hard to wrap your head around as well. As anyone who has ever gotten their taxes prepared, you can attest to the fact that that tax season is an extremely stressful time for both the taxpayer and their CPA.

Last March, we received a frantic call from a CPA we had worked with over 5 years earlier. I will call this business owner Carly. Carly called our office in the early morning hours frantic about a message that had come up on her server. We asked her to send us a picture of the message so that we could ascertain what exactly was going on. As soon as we received the email, it was crystal clear. *Ransomware.* As we dove a little deeper, we found that one of the CPA's contract employees had received a phishing email over the weekend. It seemed legitimate to her and she had clicked on the link. This one action created a chain reaction in which every single device on the network, including the server, had all files encrypted. The message on the screen was a demand for ransom in order to get their data back. Luckily Carly had a good backup of all her data on a cloud-based offsite storage solution. Even with this solution in place, it took almost 5 days to get her office back online and completely operational after the attack.

As a business owner, if you were not operational for 5 days, how much would it cost your business in lost productivity and ultimately in lost revenue?

These situations were completely different; however, there was one common denominator. The human element. The simple fact is that our employees are our strongest resource, but when not given the proper tools they can also be our greatest weakness. When it comes to Cybersecurity, business owners must put Employee Training as of our top priorities.

I talk to business owners everyday about Cybersecurity. Time and time again I find businesses that are headed for disaster. Why? Most businesses have zero training for their employees in this regard. Zero. The problem lies in the fact that the most successful attacks are being delivered daily straight to organizations just like yours through email.

Gone Phishing?

There are different types of Phishing Attacks:

Harvesting. This type of attack appears to be from a reputable company such as your bank or credit card company but is not. In this situation the end goal is to get the end user to click on the link and enter their login credentials. Once they do, unbeknownst to them, the login information has been captured.

Malware. In these attacks, malware is typically hidden in a link or in a document attachment that when clicked on launches a file to download onto the system or the network.

Ransomware. The downloaded file in these attacks will encrypt every attached device in a network. The business will be faced with a ransomware demand in order to get their data returned.

Spear-phishing. These are highly targeted attacks. Aimed at specific employees and specific organizations. The goal here is to get the person to complete a specific action, wire transfer, purchase gift cards, change banking information, etc.

Let's be crystal clear, in this new world Cyber-security Employee Training is not optional – it is a must. I am not talking about a memo to be initialed about proper Internet usage. We are talking about a multi-layered, ongoing training program for you and your staff.

One of the common misconceptions in many of the organizations that we help to support is that Cyber-security is a task or a line item for the I.T. department. This is simply just not true. Cyber-security is the responsibility of every single staff member at every level within an organization.

Do We Really Have to Train on This?

So many times, it seems like staff members should just know what to do. However, staff members are all different and they come to you from all walks of life, with different levels of education, and different levels of discernment. It is the business owners' responsibility to give them all the tools the they need to try and level the playing field. We want every single member of our team to have the ability to make the right choices when faced with the inevitable situation that could cause irreparable harm to your business.

Passwords. 81% of hacking related breaches leveraged either stolen or weak passwords.[1] In general, adults in the United States reuse the same exact password or a slight variation of that password for every application across the board. 50% of adults do not create different passwords for work and personal use.[2] We must train and require our staff to use unique passwords and that these passwords be changed every 90 days. On average, employees are sharing 6 passwords.[3] All employees must know that passwords are never to be shared and a strict policy for password management must be put in place. In other words, the "No-yellow-sticky-notes-on-your-computer-monitor-with-all-your-passwords" policy.

---

[1] 2018 Verizon Data Breach Investigation Report
[2] Last Pass 2018 Global Security Report
[3] Last Pass 2018 Global Security Report

As you can see from the list of most used passwords that password security and the need for strong passwords within organizations is real.

2018 List of Most Used Passwords According to SplashData:

1. 123456
2. Password
3. 123456789
4. 12345678
5. 12345

Administrative Access. Many organizations have all users set up with administrative rights which is problematic and could cause a great deal of damage with the occurrence of a Cyber Attack. The business owner must limit the amount of administrative rights that employees within the organization have. Then create a clearly defined policy in which employees in your company know that they are not permitted to download software without authorization. Ever. Unlicensed downloads can and will put your company at risk for an attack and could corrupt company data.

MFA (Multi Factor Authentication). We need to look at Cyber-security in layers and the more layers that we can add, the more protection (or the more difficult) we make it for cyber criminals to access our data. Multi Factor Authentication is a great tool in this regard. We need to make sure that through the training process all employees are aware that anything that they utilize that has the ability to enable MFA should be incorporated. In its simplest terms, if a password becomes compromised, a Hacker would also have to have the user's cellphone in order to gain access.

Mobile Devices. We have become such a mobile society; we have the ability to work from anywhere. With this freedom comes the need for organizations to put protocols in place for employees to follow when on the go.

1. Automate screen locking
2. Mobile devices should never be left unattended or out of one's immediate control
3. These same precautions should be taken when in the office as well

Clean Workspace Policy

Cyber-security is not always necessarily about our devices. At its core, it is about protecting confidential data from prying eyes. Within the training program that you develop for your individual organization, don't forget to include the paper trail that exists within many offices.

1. No sticky notes with password information on desk or monitor
2. Do not leave confidential information out overnight. Put all files and paperwork away at the end of each day.
3. Sensitive information should be put in a locked desk drawer during lunch and or work breaks.

Email. Email is the single most dangerous threat to every business, large and small, in the United

States right now. Most malware is delivered through email at this point. Significantly, malware that was delivered as an Office attachment rose from 5% in 2017 to 48% in 2018.[4] In this instance, the malware is delivered as a download through the macro in the document when it is opened. Employees lower their defenses for an office document and are lulled into a false sense of security.

The Most Successful Email Phishing Subject Lines[5]

1. Toll Violation Notification
2. [External] Your Unclaimed Property
3. Updated Building Evacuation Plan
4. Invoice Payment Required
5. February 2018- Updated Org Chart
6. Urgent Attention (notification of password change)

As far as Cyber-security goes, this is one of the single most important facets of Employee Training for your organization. This is where the rubber hits the road. When employees are not trained in this area the effects to your organization can be devastating.

Simulated Phishing Attacks should be part of every single organizations training plan. A simulated attack is when an email is sent to employees within an organization to see how individual employees will react, what links if any will be clicked, and if the

---

[4] Symantec 2019 Internet Threat Security Report
[5] Proofpoint 2019 State of the Phish Report

suspected threat is reported. This is a great tool to give employees real world experience with phishing attacks. One of the best ways as humans we are able to learn is through actual experience. Which is why ongoing simulated phishing attacks are so beneficial for so many organizations.

Where to Start?

When faced with the thought of creating a Cyber-security Training Program for their organization, many business owners just don't know where to begin.

We can't know where we are going without knowing where we have been. When starting the process of creating a Cyber-security Training Process for your organization, a good starting point would be to work with a Cyber-security Consultant to get a baseline for your organization. Once you have that baseline you can see exactly where you are today and work out from there.

1. Create an action plan for training your staff
2. Combine both in person and online training
3. The training absolutely must include simulated or real-world examples to be effective

Cyber-security Training for an organization is fluid, it is constantly changing, and just is not one of those areas where it is created and never revisited. One of the most important things that you can do is to open the lines of communication with your staff. You must communicate clearly both verbally and in writing what your expectations are, what the policies require them to do, and the importance of security at every level within your organization.

At the end of the day, organizations with no Cyber-security Training always have and always will suffer a greater financial loss when faced with a Cyber Attack. In the world we live in now, it isn't IF you will be attacked, you absolutely will. The question is IF you will survive and how long it will take you to recover. With proper planning, processes, and employee training, it is possible to recover with minimal disruption to your business.

Cyber-security is a war, and without providing the proper training for your employees, you will lose.

About the Author

Jeri Morgan is the President of Code Blue Computing headquartered in Denver, Colorado. Code Blue Computing is a Security First organization specializing in Cyber-security, IT Consulting, and Cloud Services. Code Blue Computing was named the 2012 Small Business of the Year by the City of Thornton, Colorado and the 2014 Emerging Business of the Year by The Broomfield Chamber of Commerce. Jeri was nominated for the Denver Business Journal Outstanding Women in Business Award in 2016 and in 2019.

A common-sense leader with a multi-faceted background in Manufacturing, Operations, and Logistics, Jeri has a knack for meeting Business Owners exactly where they are to help them build best business practices as it relates to security and utilizing technology to improve their bottom line.

Jeri can be reached as follows:

Code Blue Computing
Phone: 720-746-9763
jeri@codebluecomputing.com
http://codebluecomputing.com

Download Jeri's 5 Step Guide to Hack Proof Your Employees at www.codebluecomputing.com/employeeguide

The Real Reason For a Cyber-Security Risk Assessment

By Bart Barcewicz

What is a security assessment in business?

A cyber-security risk assessment can be compared to having a medical physical as part of your preventative healthcare. Just as most people visit their doctor on a regular basis to have their vitals checked to ensure good health, business owners should be incorporating the same practices in their business. All the various areas of your businesses need to function smoothly together, and we need to make sure all is running like a well-oiled machine. If you get an infection in your body, it could lead to dire consequences and even death. This is exactly the same for your business.

A formal Security Risk Assessment, conducted by a Cyber-security professional, is comprised of several parts. First, it identifies and assesses the risks in your business that you should be managing through your security program. It should be done annually at a minimum. There are many facets to your business; one of your employees might change or upgrade something, move your valuable data and assets to a different storage solution or even add a new platform or software. All of those come with consequences that are often not measured during changes or implementation. That is why on a regular basis you should be reviewing what is happening, then find the gaps and develop a plan to fill them.

Risk Mitigation Strategies

There are four risk mitigation strategies to be aware of. They all accomplish different results, fill certain gaps and should all be used for ALL businesses.

Risk Acceptance – you simply accept the risks as they are.

Risk Avoidance – you do whatever you can to avoid being exposed to that risk. This option is a fit for certain gaps in your business and by its very nature is also the most expensive solution.

Risk Limitation – a blend of risk acceptance and risk avoidance. This is most common.

Risk Transference – you transfer the risk to a willing third party. This is widely used for payroll services, credit card processing, etc.

There have been many breaches and hacks that originated from situations as minor as rushing a deployment of a perimeter security appliance or setting up office Wi-Fi and simply forgetting to change the default password. Hackers are always after those. Their first line to try to infiltrate a business is to scan the Internet looking for devices that allow access in the wild. Step two is to determine the type of device and then use all default passwords known to man to gain access. It is very simple for them to do this because far too many people use very basic passwords.

Why Assess Your Business Security?

As mentioned time and again in this book (but it cannot be overstated), most small business owners view being hacked or getting into problems with compliance as "I'm too small, it's not going to happen to me". Not true. In today's world we see cybercrime everywhere. There is at least one article in the news every day about a company that was breached, hacked or locked out of their data and operations. It is time to wake up and realize what I have been preaching for a while: "It is not a matter of IF but WHEN your business will be compromised by hackers."

That changes the perspective a little, doesn't it? Unfortunately, that is what it's become. Today you have to be prepared to be compromised but having all of your ducks in a row will allow your business to recover in a structured manner and avoid costly downtime or even potentially closing your doors.

Forty-one percent of companies have over 1,000 sensitive files including credit card numbers and health records left unprotected.[6]

In reality, this number is probably much higher. At my company, we see this all the time. The big problem is that most managers and business owners are not even aware of this! They have a false sense of security, thinking that a simple off-the-shelf antivirus software will protect them from cyber threats in the world today. That might have worked a long time ago, but it does not work now. Your approach to keeping your business data safe and hackers out needs to be a strategic one; a layered security approach is the way to go. To simplify, it's like an onion – you put your most valuable assets in the core and build security around it.

What happens to organizations that don't think they need a security assessment or haven't have one in a very long time?

The simple answer is – it's bad news; you can't protect against something that you have no idea is even a problem. On the other hand, if a business falls under a compliance-driven industry, such as HIPAA, then consequences are a lot worse and even criminal. Simply put, not having a security assessment performed in many cases equals being

---

[6] https://www.techrepublic.com/article/report-41-of-companies-have-1000-sensitive-files-open-to-every-employee/

hacked. Only 10% of cybercrimes are reported in the U.S. each year.[7]

What Happens When You Get Hacked?

The three worst consequences of being hacked are: irrevocably damaging your reputation, catastrophic financial loss (fines, penalties, loss of revenue and even bankruptcy) and one that most people never think about: what if the hackers never leave? This is important because you must be bullet proof after any incident that may occur. This brings us back to the start – the security assessment is crucial in order to know how to prevent the next incident from happening.

Consider this: over 80% of businesses that get hacked with ransomware and pay the ransom get hit again. Why is that? If they knew where their vulnerability was, they probably could have prevented it from happening in the first place, which means they remain vulnerable after an attack because they don't really know how it happened. Secondly, if they don't take measures to improve their security after they get hit, then it's simply negligence on their part.

---

[7] https://www.cpomagazine.com/cyber-security/11-eye-opening-cyber-security-statistics-for-2019/

What is the Right Move for You in Your Business?

After all this doom and gloom, and with so much information available on cyber-security, where should you start? Since this is your livelihood at stake, you know you must protect it but what exactly are you protecting? Data? Computers? Finances? The average businessperson does not know where to begin.

As stated, start with a security risk assessment of your business. You can do this through a cyber-security professional. Do not try to have your in-house IT person do it. A cyber-security professional is well versed in how to conduct a risk assessment because that's what they do. You pay them to find issues, holes and gaps and – trust me on this – they will. From my personal experience, there has not been a single assessment that we have done to date that didn't uncover issues. You could literally do a security assessment now, wait a month and do another one and even then, you will find risk. It's never-ending. There is literally a new threat coming every single day and it never stops. In technology, nothing is constant – it is everchanging and ever evolving more than any other element of our life.

On that note, if you hire a cyber-security professional to conduct a risk assessment and they report back that everything looks good then I can assure you that they are not the best person for the job.

They must have missed gaps and possibly were only there to collect a paycheck. Find somebody else. Check references. Get someone with at least 5 years' experience or more. Ask other business owners that you know but do not stop until you find someone good. Your business is on the line.

Step One of the Assessment

The most common way that companies are being hacked today is through email. Email = Human. Human behavior is the single weakest link in the defense of any business. But how do you assess people? It's quite simple and probably the most important task. You try to hack them. You send them a fake phishing email and see who clicks on the link, or who supplies information or even credentials. This is how a business owner can find security risks he didn't know existed. Once you discover it, then you immediately limit that risk as much as possible. You can do this by incorporating layers. Start with training (the clickers need more training). Regular training is really important. At a minimum, do it annually and provide your employees with regular mini quizzes, security tips, and so on.

The next layer goes into technical controls, meaning a solid email security solution. Not just the one that filters out spam but one that can find viruses, scan attachments before they reach your employees and even review links that come in your emails.

Your Perimeter

This is as important as email hacks. Your perimeter is essentially your exposure on the internet. Remember that once your perimeter is open, it can be reached from anywhere. What does this mean? If it is open to the internet, someone is trying to hack it. This is the world we live in now.

Internal Risks

Internal risks are just as important. There are many critical bugs that may be easily infiltrated on your internal network as well. There are many vulnerabilities on any internal network but without a proper program and assessment you can't possibly know what they are and therefore you can't fix them. Your security risk assessment will uncover these risks.

Access and data protection

Do you know which of your employees, contractors and vendors has access to what? I have seen it many times that "on paper" only certain people have access to most sensitive information, but it creates a false sense of security as it has never really been tested and the reality is often quite different. Of course, you want to trust everyone who works for you but we also must verify. Further, do you know how your employees are protecting your data? Do they send it via email, print it and leave it laying around or share with others using Dropbox? The easy way to find out is to ask them. Use a questionnaire to accomplish that.

Developing a Security Program

The most important thing you, as a business owner, can do is to choose proper security framework and review it against its controls. There are many out there like NIST, HIPAA, PCI DSS, etc. Choose the set that is the best fit for your business and then review what has been adopted as best practices in that area. Normally there are 100+ controls that should be reviewed and range from IT to HR. This is the best way to develop a security program including policies that best fit your business. Even if your business is not in a compliance-driven industry, act like it is.

After you go through the assessment, you need to determine how to prioritize what is being remediated and when it's going to happen. You should always ask your assessor to review with you the potential impact and the likelihood of the gaps/issues they have found. For example:

Number #1 – Let's say we discovered that no employee training exists and 40% of fake phishing email recipients clicked on the link or supplied information. This tells you that the likelihood of it happening is high and impact (if they download a virus) is also high. Result – take immediate action.

Number #2 – Your employees are in the habit of changing their passwords once a year and are using very strong (long) passwords. This tell you that the likelihood of any passwords being hacked is low and impact is medium so there may be other items you should take care of first.

Number #3 - We discovered that in order to efficiently do their job, your employees need to keep sensitive company information on their laptops. That makes sense but we found that their laptops are not encrypted. The likelihood of a laptop being stolen and someone accessing that information is very high, so we have to secure that immediately.

Although cyber-security is all over the news every day, and everyone knows how critical it is, it's astounding that many choose not to address it. Perhaps it's avoidance due to the mindset of "it can't happen to me." Or perhaps it's too overwhelming and frightening to think about. There are, of course, minimum-security controls that you should be implementing but you must take it upon yourself to seek out an experienced cyber-security professional to take it one step further. Your business and livelihood depend on it. Remember it is not IF but WHEN your business will become a victim to hackers. Keeping your business safe from hackers is not only a job of your security and IT vendors – it is a job for every employee in your business.

About the Author

Bart Barcewicz, a cyber-security expert, is the CEO of B Suite Cyber-security, an information security services provider. B Suite specializes in minimizing cyber breach risks for the small to mid-size businesses concerned about their reputation and digital assets. They keep business data safe and hackers out.

With industry recognized certifications in Information Security and Ethical Hacking, Bart can translate complicated cyber threats and tech issues into everyday language to easily communicate with business owners and executives. Bart prides himself on being a cutting-edge provider minimizing cyber-crime, simplifying business continuity management, finding and closing security gaps, and engineering secure networks for businesses his company serves.

B Suite Cyber-security is a leader in eliminating complexity in keeping small business data secure, and hackers out. They pride themselves on being a cutting-edge provider to minimize cyber-risk, find and close security gaps, and engineer secure-efficient networks for businesses they serve.

B Suite approaches every client the same with the same three phase approach:

1. ASSESS – It all starts there. You can't fix something you don't know exists.

2. CURE – Close all security holes and establish best in class defense programs tailored to organization's needs.

3. MAINTAIN – It's not just about a point in time security; you also have to keep your business SAFE going forward.

bb@bsuite.io
www.bsuite.io
312.600.5610
LinkedIn: https://www.linkedin.com/in/bartbarcewicz/

FREE Download
15 Security Tips Every Business Should Implement:
https://15tips.bsuite.io

Developing a Layered Security Approach

By Jason Penka

I've been working in the technology information industry for 20 years. During that time, I have seen a dramatic change in how businesses secure their data and information. At the turn of the century, business data was protected on massive servers and housed in your office, or in an office close by. Companies built dedicated server rooms and controlled access to the data from within the company network. As the internet involved, data became more distributed. Businesses started to allow employees to access that data from home, while on vacation, or working in a remote office. Information now resides in the cloud and can be accessed by anyone, anywhere, and anytime. This includes cyber criminals.

I started my company to help businesses and individual business owners protect their company data, personal information, and their clients' private information. My current company, Tech Junkies, has been working with clients for the past 12 years to help businesses manage their IT infrastructure. The past several years have seen a shift from supporting hardware, servers, workstations, and on-site backup to protecting our clients' data and providing them with business continuity in the event they have a breach or experience any data loss.

We started in a similar fashion to many other IT companies by supporting small offices and individual users. Then, over the years as word got out about our services, we started attracting larger and larger clients. Today, we service a wide range of client sizes from a single individual user all the way up to a 1,000-employee business. We focus the majority of our efforts on working with compliance-driven industries such as medical offices, hospitals, medical support vendors, financial institutions, banks, and government agencies. Over the years we have found that the same levels of security needed for large compliance-driven industries still need to be in place for smaller companies. Small businesses, and the employees that run them, are a huge target for cyber criminals. They are considered the 'low hanging fruit' of the cyber-criminal world.

Several years ago, we started getting calls from small businesses and individual business owners that had been hit with ransomware, major viruses, and malicious software that was rendering their business inoperable. These events were destroying businesses and lives.

I'd like to share a real-life example with you. We were contacted by a local insurance company, located in Central Kansas, that employed over 40 people in their offices. The company was going through another growth period and was looking at adding more employees to their current office and also opening a second office about an hour away. They requested that my company come in to assess their current infrastructure, future needs, and provide a quote for remediation. We started this process like hundreds before and began performing a deep Network and Security Audit. We installed software on their network, workstations, and server to pull data and find any issues that might be lurking. We compiled the report and sat down with the senior leadership to discuss our findings and provide a solution.

Here is what we found. They were using several different IT companies to support their network. Specifically, they had a remote-only IT company based in Florida to support the four servers in their main office. This Florida firm was responsible for keeping the servers up and running to avoid any downtime for the employees. They did this by providing support remotely. When they needed a physical person on site, they hired a local company.

This local company was responsible for the backup of the data on these servers. They installed their own hardware appliance in the server room to do so. This device performed the backups of the server and sent the data to an off-site data center; however, the owners of the company did not know where that data center was located. According to their contract, the backups were checked each day and the email was sent to their server support company in Florida.

For their network, they hired a local internet service provider to handle the physical network equipment and management of the firewall. The local ISP had the best of intentions, but they were not equipped to handle a client of this size. Their local firewall was simply an 'off the shelf' router they purchased at Best Buy. Their network equipment consisted of what we call in the industry unmanaged switches or "dumb switches". Basically, it just means that you plug in the network cables and they distribute the internet similar to how a power strip is plugged in and distributes power.

Since they had a large client service area, most of the employees had laptops they used at work and took home at the end of the day. These laptops were supported by a single person inside the company who was also the company's CFO. This is what we call a 'slash' position and we see this a lot in IT. When a company grows quickly and needs someone to "be in charge of IT," they just add the role to an existing member of the staff. This is what happened to the CFO. He was in charge of buying equipment, finding vendors, and supporting their local users when they had questions. He was thrown into this position with little to no training.

We found that their servers were being patched (updated) properly, but their back up system was not functioning properly 100% of the time, their network equipment and "firewall" (the off the shelf router from Best Buy) was shockingly inadequate for their security needs, and their local work-stations had ZERO protection against any major viruses. (To be fair, they had installed Norton antivi-rus on the computers, but this is NOT considered a business class anti-virus software).

After describing the issues that we found, we dis-cussed our fee for remediation and on-going sup-port. This was dramatically higher than they were currently paying. We explained that this was due to the fact that they had not been properly funding their IT needs for the last 7 years that they were in business. We expressed our understanding that this can be a shock to the system, but it is what was truly needed at this point in their company.

They decided to think about it and get back to us. We scheduled a follow up for a week later and left the meeting. Two months went by. Then we get a call. They were hit with a ransomware attack. All of their company laptops and servers were encrypted and the hackers were asking for a ransom. The hackers were demanding $50,000 in bitcoin. We asked about their backups. We were told that their local backups were affected by the ransomware. This also spread to their off-site backups because the system was just put together by the company that was supporting it and not designed or hardened against this type of account (this was something we had discussed in their meeting). The kicker on this was that their employees did a lot of work at home and in-home offices. Many of them, especially the senior staff, had a full workstation at home that was separate from their company laptop. They stored a large number of important files at home on these home computers. However, because their company laptops were on the same network as their home computers the virus has spread itself to their home computers as well before being deployed. As a result, many employees even had their personal family computers locked by the ransomware.

They were basically dead in the water at this point. The only step from here was to pay the ransom. We offered to help with the process, but their CFO was up to speed enough with bitcoin that he opted to handle the transaction. They paid the ransom to the cyber criminals and received the decryption code. They entered the decryption code on the first server.... nothing. It didn't work. They tried several other servers, workstations, and laptops and it still didn't work. At this point they were out $50,000, lost all of the company data, and the majority of the employees lost their personal files, photos, and videos on their home computers. Within three months, the company was bankrupt and closed for business.

I tell this story not to highlight a company that did everything wrong or to blame the company, the owners, or the IT vendors. This happened because they were not taking an ongoing layered approach to their IT and cyber-security needs. The old saying goes, "You can only eat an elephant one bite at a time." Now, this company was in a critical situation when they came to us. They NEEDED to eat that entire elephant all at once and we were more than capable of helping. But they didn't realize how far behind they were and that catching up was going to be more like ripping a band-aid off. You can't let this happen to your business.

It is a matter of WHEN not IF your business will experience a cyber-attack. This can come in the form of a malicious email, ransomware, direct attack, or social engineering. The methods to attack your business are many and varied. You have to be prepared to volley these attacks or avoid them altogether. The best method to approach this is by having a layered security approach to your cyber-security and IT infrastructure plan. This allows you to focus on what is important right now and plan for additional protection in the future so you can scale your IT needs properly to match emerging threats. The biggest benefit to a layered approach is that you aren't relying on just a single point of failure to protect your business. In the following section, I'm going to outline the facts of cyber-crime, what it means to your company, what a layered security approach looks like, and the next steps you need to take.

As we have all mentioned in every chapter of this book, if you think, "My company is small, so I won't be a target" you're dead wrong. Small to mid-sized businesses accounted for 62% of all cyber-attacks.[8] Cyber-attacks for small businesses are getting more sophisticated and more malicious. Ransomware has seen a 90% increase in Q1 of 2019.[9] A business is falling victim to a ransomware attack every 14 seconds.[10] According to the U.S. National Cyber-security Alliance 60% of small businesses attacked are unable to sustain their business 6 months after the attack.[11]

These stats can be extremely concerning and downright scary. With all of the reports in the news of large companies, government agencies, large cities, and major hospitals being breached, it may seem like there isn't any hope for you as a small business owner. You'd be wrong! The reason those larger agencies have been breached is due to a combination of not taking their cyber-security defense seriously and being targeted by cyber criminals. As a small business owner, you need to ensure you are reducing your threat profile and not being one of the 'low hanging fruit.'

---

[8] "Hacked: The Implications of a Cyber Breach" Timothy Francis, enterprise lead for Cyber insurance - https://www.propertycasualty360.com/2015/05/27/small-mid-sized-businesses-hit-by-62-of-all-cyber/

[9] Coveware's Q1 Ransomware Marketplace Report - https://www.coveware.com/blog/2019/4/15/ransom-amounts-rise-90-in-q1-as-ryuk-ransomware-increases

[10] Cybersecurity Ventures - https://cybersecurityventures.com/cybersecurity-almanac-2019/

[11] https://www.inc.com/joe-galvin/60-percent-of-small-businesses-fold-within-6-months-of-a-cyber-attack-heres-how-to-protect-yourself.html

Cyber criminals are able to automate their attacks. They have farms of computers operating every second of every day doing nothing but looking for vulnerabilities in open networks. They don't know who they are attacking just that they can attack them. Taking a layered approach is going to greatly reduce your threat profile and make you a much harder target. To get started, I suggest you take the following steps and apply the necessary layers to start protecting your business.

Your Layered Security Approach in 7 Steps

1. Perimeter Protection – If you think of protecting your company's network like you would protect a house, the perimeter protection would be the fence around your house. The fence won't let anyone or anything in without permission. For your business, this 'fence" is your email. You need to have an enterprise level filter on your email that scans incoming email for SPAM, Malware, and any other malicious files. Ninety-two percent of malware is delivered through email. In fact, 38% of malicious attacks are masked as a Microsoft Office file type. These files are sent through email for business purposes every day. To start, I recommend you host your email through Microsoft Office 365 and utilize a Microsoft Partner to do so. Out of the box Office 365 is not configured securely and the responsibility lies on every company to handle the configuration for themselves. There are certified

Microsoft Partners in a nationwide network that can provide you secure hosted email through Office 365 that will include enterprise level SPAM protection, multi-factor authentication, and even backup and email recovery solutions in the event your email is compromised. These services are usually priced per user and aren't much more than what you pay to receive the software directly from Microsoft. I believe it to be money well spent.

2. Edge – Unified Threat Management / Firewall – Going back to our previous house analogy, an enterprise class Unified Threat Management (UTM) device (commonly called a Firewall), would be the home security system that is monitoring everything coming through the fence, checking it against intruders, and alerting you to threats. It will then prevent those threats from entering the house by locking the door. As mentioned previously, not all firewalls are created the same; buying any firewall or router off the shelf at the store won't do the trick. The best-in-class firewalls need to be constantly managed and maintained. They receive regular updates, so they know when new threats are present in the environment. The "out-of-the-box" solutions are not configured as such. I suggest you reach out to an IT Security Professional to seek assistance with finding a firewall brand, model, and size that will work best for your company. Some best in class companies providing enterprise level firewalls are: Sophos, Cisco, Palo Alto, Fortinet, or SonicWall. Most of these hardware providers will require you to work with an IT partner for installation.

3. Endpoint – Next Generation Anti-Virus and Web Filtering – Not all anti-virus protection solutions are created equal. There has been a huge shift in the anti-virus market in the past 12 months. What has emerged is being called Next Generation anti-virus. Previous anti-virus companies have a very simple model: they sell you the software, you install the software, then they send updates to the software daily and the software scans the computer looking for files that look bad based on a list of known threats the anti-virus company has developed. If they see a file run that fits the profile of a threat according to their list, they will attempt to block the file. In most cases, the virus is already installed, and the user has just been notified of an issue. The problem with this model is it focuses on "reacting-and-responding" when a virus is found. It doesn't take into account how fast viruses are changing in the wild. Traditional anti-virus applications just can't keep up anymore. In contrast, Next Generation anti-virus focuses on looking for files that act like a malicious piece of software and prevents it from running at all. Next Generation anti-virus changes the delivery model as well. The software is installed on a computer and is then managed, monitored, and maintained by an IT Professional. This puts a "guard in the tower" to watch for anything that seems out of place. This Next Generation anti-virus is not being provided by the well-known names in the marketplace. Norton,

MacAfee, BitDefender, and Webroot do NOT have a solution that is considered to be Next Generation. The products we work with are from Sophos, SentialOne, and DeepInstinct, which are companies that are, more than likely, not known by the average business owner.

4. Business Continuity – Business continuity is like having insurance on your home. In the event that something catastrophic happens, you can be made whole again by your insurance or in the case of your IT, your backup system. A true business continuity plan revolves around a few key factors: backing up data to a local device, virtualizing your servers/workstation on that device, sending entire imaged-based copies of your backup off-site daily, testing those local backups, and testing the off-site backup. A good rule of thumb to follow is: If the backup can't be verified, then it doesn't exist. There are various products on the market that provide data backup and business continuity. I suggest speaking with an IT Professional and have them walk you through the process of finding the right backup for your business needs. This will depend on the number of servers you have, the amount of data to backup, and the amount of time you can be down in the event of data loss. We have a standard policy of 1 hour of downtime for our clients. We have several clients that have a lower threshold and need that downtime reduced to minutes. In these cases, we build custom continuity programs for them to achieve that goal. Make sure you are getting verification that your backup has been performed successfully. This will come in the form of email verification and screenshots of your server running in a virtual environment. Ensure your provider is performing at least monthly test restores on the hardware virtualization and weekly test restores on the cloud storage solution. Business continuity is generally not something a small business owner can do in-house. It is best to hire an IT Professional to set it up and monitor it for you.

5. Internal Considerations – Multi-factor Authentication, Password Management, User Training, and Network Monitoring – This is similar to in-home security you have in your house: locks on the doors, locks on the windows, running fire drills, motion detectors, a built-in safe, and maybe even a gun under your pillow. Multi-factor authentication goes a long way to reduce your threat landscape. This adds a second step to your login process when you log in to websites and services you use on a daily basis. The premise is that it allows the website to send you a notification via text message, phone call, unique device, or phone app that verifies that it is in fact you logging into the website. This prevents cyber criminals from logging into websites as you even if they have stolen your credentials. Password management solutions also provide a secure method to store your passwords. Since the passwords are stored and automatically entered into the website, it is easier to utilize complex secure passwords. Having a password like Password12345 is easy to remember for you but it is also easy for a cyber-criminal to hack. Having a password like *U&i9e#@87qA is hard to remember but also hard to crack for a criminal. Password managers will help you remember those passwords and keep them safe and secure. Just like overhead expenses, cyber breaches walk on two legs. Providing ongoing training for your staff can help prevent a wide range of cyber-attacks. If your employees know what to look for, they will know when to report suspicious activity. Internal network monitoring can be performed on enterprise class network switches. This allows your IT Professional to monitor the network traffic to look for malicious software that might be trying to call home from inside your network.

6. Fighting Back – Cyber-security Intelligence – New companies are emerging that will help you detect threat activity in real-time, drive it away, and find out how it got in. This is akin to the barking dog in your yard. If something doesn't seem right, the dog chases it down and scares it away. Cyber-security intelligence companies track the threat back to where it came in through the fence and show you where your breach occurred. This provides yet another extra layer of insurance. Some security threats aren't your fault or the fault of your IT provider; a vulnerable piece of software could have left the door open. Advanced Threat Detection will help stop the threat in its tracks, plug the hole, report on the issue, and provide remediation solutions.

7. Cyber Liability Insurance – Just like backup, your business needs a true Cyber Liability and Cyber Crime Insurance policy. The key with cyber liability insurance is you have to show you are taking steps to keep your network secure for the policy to be enforceable. Just like you can't start campfires in your living room and collect insurance when your house burns down, you can't expect cyber liability insurance to pay in the event of a breach if you haven't taken steps to protect your network. The insurance company will probably sell you the insurance; the kicker comes when you have a breach and they find you were at fault.

The bottom line is that small business owners need to take cyber-security and protecting their company's and client's data very seriously. Is it an additional expense? Yes. But the threat is real and it could be crippling to your business if you don't act on it now. When we first engage with a new client, we start with a Cyber-security Self-Assessment. This walks them through a simple test that will provide them with a score for their security of their business. I have made this form available on our website at https://www.thetechjunkies.net/hack proof. Along with the self-assessment tool, I am also including a 30-minute strategy call with me directly. We can review the results of the assessment, answer any questions you have, and provide you with the critical next steps.

About the Author

Jason Penka is a technology entrepreneur and Founder of CEO of Tech Junkies and Residential MSP Group both headquartered in Hays, Kansas. Serving Western Kansas since 2007, Tech Junkies focuses on servicing residential and small to midsized businesses with general IT management and cyber-security solutions. Residential MSP Group is Jason's most recent business venture.

Jason grew in a family of entrepreneurs and small business owners with companies ranging from retail to professional services. Unlike most IT business owners, Jason wanted to ensure those small business owners weren't left out when it came to utilizing technology. This led Jason to create a program within Tech Junkies called CloudCare Secure™. This program provides home and small business clients with enterprise class technology and cyber-security solutions at an affordable price.

After creating a truly unique service delivery model for technology and cyber-security solutions to residential and small offices through Tech Junkies, Jason founded Residential MSP Group (rMSP). rMSP is focused on helping other IT companies expand their businesses utilizing the CloudCare Secure™ program.

During college at Fort Hays State University he found his passion for business through leadership and entrepreneurship classes and projects. As a final project in his degree program Jason developed a business plan for a web development company. This plan would end up being the source material for what would become Tech Junkies. The plan was so well developed it was used as a template for the class going forward.

Jason enjoys working with small and midsized businesses to develop a technology plan that will help keep their company secure, help them reduce wasted time, and implement innovative technology. He serves on several local boards and committees including the Informatics Advisory Council at his alma mater FHSU.

When not helping people and businesses with technology, he can be found on the golf course, cooking, or attending a rock concert.

jason@thetechjunkies.net
www.linkedin.com/in/jasonpenka
www.thetechjunkies.net
785-621-2445
https://www.facebook.com/OfficialJasonPenka

Preventing Hacks With a Technology Success Plan

By Ross Brouse

American writer and professor, Isaac Asimov, once said, "The saddest aspect of life right now is that science gathers knowledge faster than society gathers wisdom."

It was a Thursday afternoon in September 2015 when John, our main point of contact at a local small business messaged me and said, "I cannot open files on the file server. They seem to be corrupt!" "Hold on a minute while I check", I replied. At the time, I was the primary technical resource for this client, so it was customary for me to be personally responding to a message like this. As I logged into the file server, I was presented with that message that nobody ever wants to see... Ooops, your important files are encrypted. None of our clients had ever been the victim of a ransomware attack before but I had heard about this message and knew what it meant. Like the feeling you get when you suddenly realize you've lost your child in a crowded mall, panic struck. What should I do next? Who do I tell and how do I explain this? What happens if all of their data is lost? As these thoughts blazed through my mind, I had to inform John, "There is an issue with the file server. All files are corrupt. You've been infected with a ransomware virus."

The next 48 hours were challenging. Our antivirus engine could not have stopped this attack and the lack of end-user training also helped to make the attack possible. Fortunately, in 2015, time bomb ransomware was not yet prevalent and as a result, our backups from 2 days prior were still good. We managed to restore the file server within 48 hours and despite data being a day and a half old, the client was quickly back up and running. After any kind of technology-based incident like this one, the question everyone always asks is, "How could this have been prevented?"

My name is Ross Brouse and I am the President & Chief Operating Officer of Continuous Networks. We are a New Jersey based Technology Success Practice that specializes in small business technology strategy planning and implementation. We service clients in the manufacturing, wholesale, import/export, medical and dental spaces. Our mission is to enrich the lives of our people, our clients and our families by creating outstanding business results through technology. We achieve our mission by utilizing a unique business-focused approach to technology support that mitigates risk, improves employee efficiency, evaluates business impact and reduces overall technology spend. We work to replace a "reactive mindset" with forward thinking, strategy-based processes that are essential to the business success we build for our clients. We prevent our clients from getting hacked by implementing what we call the "Continuous Standard", which is a set of standards that achieve overall technology success and not only prevent hacks but realize significantly better business outcomes.

How Could This Have Been Prevented?

How could that attack on John's company have been prevented? Perhaps if we'd had a better anti-virus tool? Maybe if we'd had more monitoring in place? Possibly a higher quality firewall with a more advanced feature set? The problem with this line of thinking is that it is a reaction to an incident that has already occurred. George Bernard Shaw once said, "The possibilities are endless once we decide to act and not react." The beauty of acting instead of reacting, is that we have the opportunity to plan for a disaster. Reacting to an incident after it has already happened forces an emotional response to loss aversion. Our mind is clouded by frustration, anger and fear. In this state, we simply cannot make logical decisions that further our goals in an efficient and intelligent way. While everything is running smoothly, we have the ability to calmly and rationally make smart business decisions that improve our position on the strategic technology map. We stop to consider things like risk, business impact, productivity and efficiency. We work with our peers to make better decisions and develop processes that are designed to create stability and resilience within our organizations. Most simply stated, we are prepared!

Why don't more companies make a conscious decision to be prepared with their technology processes? I was thinking in very simple terms when I first asked myself this question. The answer I arrived at was: Money. Companies simply don't want to spend the money, I thought. When I'd meet with potential clients and we'd have this conversation, very few saw the value in spending money to prevent a problem that had never happened to them before. I'd demonstrate the risks and even cite specific examples that were relevant to their business. Nothing worked! Everyone was "FINE" and would say things like, "We're too small", "These hackers aren't interested in my business" or even "I hear you and I am concerned about it, but I just can't afford that right now...". I'd walk away from these conversations, scratching my head and wondering what I had done wrong. Why don't these businesses want to protect themselves from loss? I would think to myself.

About 10 years ago, my insurance broker sat down with me to discuss my company's health insurance policy. My oldest daughter was 3 at the time and I had recently purchased a home. He slid a whole life insurance illustration toward me across the desk as he said, "Ross. Before we discuss your health policy, I want to talk with you about life insurance. It's time you start thinking more about your future." He went on to tell me how it was important that I left my family with a proper financial plan in the untimely event of my demise. The illustration that he presented walked through a whole life policy that was paid up until age 99 and it showed me how the money I would spend on a monthly basis would grow over time. I'd never really looked into whole life insurance policies before, but I knew they were expensive! "How can you expect me to spend all this money every month?" I said to him. He sat there for a moment, his eyes transfixed on me, thinking about how to choose his words carefully. "Ross. I hate to put it this way, but if you died tomorrow... how would your wife pay the mortgage?" he stated with a commonsensical tone. I paused for a few moments and then responded back, "Honestly. I don't know. I hadn't thought about that before." Over the next several minutes, he explained the coverage I would receive from the policy in addition to the cash value that would grow progressively. He continued on to show me how I could use that cash over time and how the monthly payment I would contribute to the policy was truly an investment in my future. "You'll sleep better at night, knowing your family is protected.", he said to me before he left. The million-dollar question is, since I've never died before, why did I choose to spend money on a whole life insurance policy?

As Benjamin Franklin said in his 1789 letter to Jean-Baptiste Leroy, "But in this world nothing can be said to be certain, except death and taxes." I'd like to adapt Benjamin Franklin's quote to say, "in the world of business, nothing is certain but death, taxes and getting hacked." As I attended more appointments and had more conversations with business owners and business leaders, it began to dawn on me that the real issue was that most business owners came into work every morning and went home every night, without any incident. Like your life, if you wake up every day, your expectation is that you will wake up again tomorrow as well. The problem wasn't that companies wouldn't spend the money on protecting themselves from loss, but that I simply had not shown them how they could leverage the money they did spend to create a better result. Like my life insurance policy, the service I was offering to my clients needed to pay dividends! I had spent all of these years fixing computers and dealing with technical support requests, only to discover that I now had to become a business consultant!

I soon adopted software and systems that allowed my staff to align our customers with best practices and standards and I began to assemble a plan for the quarterly meetings with my clients. Rather than showing a client how quickly we responded to their requests or how many requests we serviced in the previous 3 months, I started to utilize tools to present the weaknesses within their technology and show how those weaknesses could impact their business. We started to analyze what the issues were and where they came from so that we could strategize on how to prevent those issues from happening in the first place. Then we went about creating processes around those weaknesses so that those weaknesses would become strengths. Over time, we started to see the number of support incidents decrease, which allowed us to use our time proactively and focus on the bigger goals for each company's technology. Our quarterly meetings truly became strategy sessions where we would plan major projects and talk about business growth and optimization. What was once a stressful 60 minutes of digging into why things didn't work became a positive and productive planning process for building a better business.

Why do so many businesses suffer these attacks? In short, because they fail to plan. Once again, as the great Benjamin Franklin said, "If you fail to plan, you are planning to fail!" Our firm helps small businesses prevent cyber-attacks through proper strategic planning and implementation of a technology success plan.

What does a technology success plan look like and how do you implement it?

A proper technology success plan does not have to be complicated. In fact, it should be easy! Our plan is a 5-phase process that we call the "Continuous Track". Each phase is designed to reach a specific milestone towards technology success. Not only does this plan greatly mitigate your risk of a cyber-attack, but it also ensures you have a proper data backup and restoration process, helps you build an effective disaster response process and significantly reduces general technology support issues that cost you money! For the purpose of our topic, let's focus on how a technology success plan, like the Continuous Track, can help you and your business prevent cyber-attacks.

Phase 1: Secure

Start with backups! A proper backup strategy and infrastructure is a critical component of your technology success plan. Most companies think it's enough to run backups to an external hard drive or possibly even a third party cloud. I've even seen numerous companies who use an overly complex rotating external hard drive system and the IT manager or CEO will periodically take these drives home with them. While I understand the desire to want your backups off-site, this is NOT the way to achieve it!

You must utilize a tiered backup strategy that provides multiple restore points and locations. This type of approach helps to mitigate situations where your backups become compromised. A proper RPO (Recovery Point Objective) is also necessary so that you know how much data you are storing, how often you are backing it up and where you are keeping it. It's not enough just to run backups, you also must restore those backups so that you can be sure they work. Additionally, those restores become fire drills for the real thing. Now you can prove that not only is it possible to restore your data, but also how long it takes. It's important to test your tiered backup system both on-site and in the cloud, to be sure everything works as well as your backup and restoration plan states. Record the results and use that data to measure your backup and restoration processes over time.

Next comes installing the proper monitoring and security tools. These days, most IT vendors you will speak with have a good handle on these types of tools. The vendors who sell these tools make it really easy to purchase and they will sell to anyone calling themselves a technology provider. In fact, with a few thousand dollars in your pocket, you could go purchase most of these tools and launch your own technology support company out of the basement of your house! It's important to understand "WHY" your IT vendor chose the tools they are using and how those tools are going to get your business, better results.

Some of the important "WHY" security tools requirements are:

- Monitoring tools will alert your IT vendor, 24/7/365 of critical downtime and performance related alerts

- Security and monitoring tools do not have single points of failure

- Security tools are monitored 24/7/365 by trained security professionals who will remediate threats in real-time

- Security tools are tiered, providing protection at multiple levels of the technology stack including the perimeter, the network, workstations, servers, printers and any IoT device

- Security and monitoring tools do not become useless once as device leaves the corporate network

- Security tools can properly measure and report data that can be understood by a businessperson

Phase 2: Engage

One of the most important aspects of building a technology success plan is to engage with the people using the technology. In order to engage with users successfully, you must know the answers to these questions:

- How do your employees perform their daily work and what types of devices do they utilize?

- Do your employees work remotely and if so, what is required in order for them to efficiently and securely perform their job functions?

- Are your employees trained on proper security processes and protocols regarding the use of mobile devices and data?

- Are your employees given annual training on how to identify cyber-attacks coming from email, text messages and web sites?

- Does your company leverage regular phish testing processes so that you can identify weaknesses within your employee base?

- Does your company maintain accurate documentation on permission and access controls for various departments and users?

- Does your company utilize user behavior analytics (UBA) tools to identify and report on anomalous behavior?

Once you understand how your users interact with and use your company's technology systems, set up security training requirements to be sure that users are armed with the required knowledge to protect both themselves and your company. Organize regular training sessions and then frequently test your employee base to be sure they are meeting your security standards. Build the necessary processes and policies around the use of mobile devices and data security and then require your employees to sign-off on these policies to be sure they understand them and will comply with them. Deploy the necessary tools and systems to monitor and report on user behavior across your employee base and then review and analyze that data regularly. You must properly manage, train and equip your employees as they are your company's greatest strength and its greatest weakness in the fight against cyber-attacks.

Phase 3: Analyze

Meet with your IT vendor and begin by choosing a set of best practices and standards. Whether its COBIT, ITIL, NIST or some other set of standards, take the time to evaluate your technology infrastructure against the standards you have chosen. How does your technology stack up and what are your weak points? Identify where you are weak and then analyze and utilize the data you collected within the Engage phase to build out an execution plan. This execution plan should consist of quarterly strategic goals that address the weak points within your technology stack. Prioritize these strategic goals and concentrate on the issues that create the greatest impact to the business first. If you are able to identify low or no cost items that have a significant positive impact, add those to the top of your list.

Don't just plan to spend money. Building out and following documented processes is the key to protecting your business from a cyber-attack. Start discussing and collecting data to build out your core technology success processes including:

- Data backup and recovery

- Passwords and permissions

- Mobile Device and Bring Your Own Device (BYOD)

- Single Sign On and multi-factor authentication

- Data security and use

- Disaster response and recovery

Phase 4: Execute

It is important that you have well defined roles and responsibilities for your execution plan. At our firm, we call these roles the Continuous Alignment Manager and the Continuous Business Strategist. The Alignment Manager's job is to continuously evaluate your technology stack against the best practices and standards you have chosen. The results of this regular process must then be evaluated against the overall business goals and key initiatives. The Business Strategist's job is to fully understand your business so they can help you properly prioritize the items within your execution plan. Working with these two key individuals, come to an agreement on your execution plan deliverables and timeline before implementation and then carry out your plan. Always follow the standards you have chosen while making sure to stop and measure your progress and performance at periodic intervals. This phase is not meant to be accomplished quickly. Executing on your overall technology success plan is a discipline that will take place every quarter.

Phase 5: Dedicate

Don't stop. Technology Success is not "set it and forget it". You must continuously evaluate your technology success plan and re-prioritize your quarterly key initiatives when required. Cyber criminals are shrewd businesspeople who are committed to invading your company's network. If you do not continuously evaluate, prioritize and execute on your technology success plan, these cyber criminals will gain the edge over you and your company. Remain dedicated to learning about emerging threats and how they may affect you. Work with a competent security focused technology vendor who understands that protecting you is a long-term discipline. This vendor should regularly report on your technology success grade and what your plan and budget looks like for at least 4 quarters in advance. Additionally, they should consistently report on remediated threats to your network and data along with the findings of your backup and recovery testing. Building a cadence and discipline around these efforts will vastly improve the safety and security of your network and data.

A Technology Success Plan is Your Defense Against Cyber Threats

When I meet with small businesses to discuss their technology risk and exposure, I typically find that most business leaders do not have a good understanding of cyber-crime and how these criminals mount their attacks. "That will never happen to me", "We're too small to get attacked" and "It's a risk I am willing to take" are things I hear from business leaders often. The fact is, cyber criminals do not target big companies or small companies. These bad actors cast a wide net and do not discriminate based on company size or industry. They are businesspeople who are well trained in their craft and because of the lack of knowledge and planning throughout the SMB market today, they are wildly successful. To them, every business's data is worth stealing, including yours! According to Boston Security Network, 60% of companies that lose their data go out of business within 6 months. That's a very scary statistic and it's one that should be taken very seriously. Building a cyber defense strategy with a technology success plan is your best defense against the continuously changing threat landscape.

Remember John and the ransomware attack that nearly destroyed all of his company's data? Today, John has a bullet proof technology success plan that maintains an extremely high level of security for his company. Rather than reacting to threats, John and his company spend their time planning and preventing them. They sleep better at night knowing that they've invested the time and the resources necessary to protect themselves and if required, can rely on their plan to remediate a disaster. John works with his dedicated alignment manager and business strategist to continuously evaluate their technology success grade and make improvements where necessary. John and his company get predictable outcomes and there are no unplanned costs. In fact, John's company spends less money per employee today while having significantly better security than they did before they started to plan and strategize. Follow John's lead and implement a well-built technology success plan for your business. It is the best way to not only protect yourself from threats but also to reduce overall technology spend across your organization.

About the Author

Ross Brouse has been practicing his geeky techno-wizardry since the late 1990s. Ross attended New York University Tisch School of the Arts and graduated with a degree in Film and Television production in 2000. After college he helped build a graphic design business with his colleagues from NYU and Cooper Union. Ross's entrepreneurial spirit led him to go solo and build two of his own businesses, one of which became a predecessor to Continuous Networks. Ross has a fanatical passion

for mastering technologies and providing customers with an IT experience that is second to none.

t. 973-572-1069
m. 973-202-9000
www.continuous.net
Secaucus, NJ

Download Ross's 7 Most Critical
IT Security Protections Report

https://www.continuous.net/7-most-critical-
it-security-protections

Social Engineering, Spear-phishing, Whaling, and How Not to Be a Victim

By Bill Bunnell

You're sitting at your desk and you receive an email from your bank and it is serious; someone is attempting to log into your business bank account. You immediately panic and react. You ask yourself, What are they doing? Are they trying to withdraw all the money? You click on the link in the email and follow the instructions. You enter the username and password to your bank account. BAM! Instantly, you and your company just became a victim of a social engineering cyber-attack. You just gave the hackers full access to your business bank. The hackers immediately start transferring all of your business' money to bank accounts which they control.

As an IT professional with over 20 years of industry experience, this is typically how a cyber-attack happens. You have no idea that you have become a victim of a cyber-attack until it is too late. As a business owner, you need to be educated on how to identify and prevent becoming a victim of such attacks. As CEO of Network Builders IT, my job, along with my team, is to provide IT support and security services to businesses. Our mission is to protect businesses and their end-users from cyber-security incidents by providing them with advanced security tools and, most importantly, educating end-users on how to identify malicious emails and websites. To properly protect a business from cyber threats, multiple layers of security best practices and tools need to be implemented. Over time, the security tools and software have become so advanced that hackers have turned to social engineering as the main attack vector. By nature, people are very trusting and easy to trick; hackers know this and take full advantage of it. Because of this, end-user training has become a critical component in protecting businesses from cyber-attacks. The most common method used to carry out a social engineering-based cyber-attack against a business is through emails sent to end-users. For end-users to better protect themselves and the business, they must know what a social engineering email looks like and what to do when one is discovered.

In today's corporate world of email and online commerce, it is common to become a victim. Social engineering is the most effective weapon hackers have, and they are taking full advantage of it. So, what do we do, how do we protect ourselves, how do you know if the emails you receive are real or not? These are the questions I will answer.

Social Engineering and Phishing Defined

Why are Social Engineering and Phishing such potent tools for hackers? Many people think that phishing emails are only a problem if you get fooled into providing your credentials. This just isn't true. Simply by clicking on one link in a malicious email, your computer can be completely compromised. In recent research conducted by Duo, a part of Cisco, 31% of people click on phishing links, and 17% of people enter credentials on phishing sites. In addition to users easily being tricked by these malicious emails, according to Symantec's 2018 Internet Security Threat Report, 54.6% of all email is spam.

Furthermore, the data shows that the average user receives 16 malicious spam emails per month. The math is scary; if a company only had 20 employees, the employees would need to correctly identify and deal with 3,840 malicious emails over one year. The threat is real, and businesses are being targeted and attacked. To add to the confusion, the IT industry has attached strange names to threats such as Social Engineering, Phishing, Spear phishing, and Whaling, to name just a few. Let's start by defining what all these terms mean.

Social Engineering

It all starts with Social Engineering, which is the art of deception used to manipulate people into providing confidential or personal information. Social Engineering takes many different forms from emails to phone calls. The goal is to gain trust or sound authoritative and trick you into providing personal and confidential information. I am sure most of us have received phone calls claiming to be the IRS or Microsoft tech support claiming there is a problem with your computer. The same techniques are being used to attack businesses and trick employees.

Phishing – not only via email

Phishing is a general term for using social engineering via email to exploit users. Like casting a large net in the hopes of catching something, most phishing attacks send emails to thousands if not millions of email addresses. The attackers know that there is a low chance that the recipient will take the bait, but because of the large number of recipients, someone is bound to take that bait and become a victim. Be aware that phishing attacks are not only limited to emails; your users can be attacked via social media, phone calls (called "vishing" for voice-phishing) and text messages (called "smishing" for SMS-phishing). Identifying phishing can be very difficult for the average person because the hackers are very good at making them look legitimate! If you want to test you and your employees' skills in detecting phishing, Google.com has provided an online test that users can take. I encourage you to take a minute and test your skills. The quiz is located here https://phishingquiz.withgoogle.com/

Spear-phishing

Spear-phishing is the most common type of cyber-attack that we see in the business environment. This is a targeted attempt to steal sensitive information such as account credentials or financial information from a specific victim such as an Accounting staff member or Administrative assistant, often for malicious reasons. Hackers will research a company and its employees by reviewing the information available on Facebook, LinkedIn, or even the company website to acquire details about the intended victim, such as their email address and their position in the company. The attackers then disguise themselves as a trustworthy person to acquire sensitive information. Often, we see emails where it looks like the CEO is emailing the CFO or an assistant asking for something to be done.

In one real example of a spear-phishing attack, a fake email from the CEO was sent to an administrative assistant asking for several hundreds of dollars of iTunes gift cards to be purchased. The assistant was to email back the redemption code on the back of the card. In this particular attack, the email stated that the CEO was unavailable by phone, but needed the codes as quickly as possible. The victim, thinking the email was legitimate and from a trusted source, followed the instructions without question. It was not until much later that it was discovered to be a cyber-attack. In another real example, an HR department admin received an email request to modify an employee's direct deposit information. This actually happens very frequently. In this instance, the HR department changed the employee's direct deposit information based on instructions provided in the email. It was not until the employee noticed that they had not received their paycheck that this cyber-attack was discovered.

Because people are trusting by nature, spear-phishing works extremely well. It is the most successful form of acquiring confidential information on the internet, accounting for 91% of attacks according to Cofense research. Businesses must train their employees on what to look for and implement new processes to prevent these types of cyber-attacks. Hiring an outside IT professional is the best route to take because they work in the field and can provide valuable training.

Whaling

A whaling attack is a targeted attempt to steal highly sensitive data from a company such as personal details about employees or financial information. In whaling attacks, senior management such as the CEO or CFO is typically the target of these targeted attacks. It's called whaling because the hacker is going after the "big whale" at the company. While the techniques used in whaling attacks are in general the same as other phishing attacks, what makes these different is the relative importance of the target and their access and authority to sensitive company information. The goal, like all phishing attacks, is to trick the executive into revealing data that they would otherwise not disclose to a stranger.

Whaling attacks can be more difficult to detect because they appear to come from a trusted source and are highly personalized towards the target, including names, titles and other details to make the communication look legitimate. Typically, the email will even have details such as company logos, phone numbers and spoofed email addresses to make them seem like they are originating from a trusted source. They are often extremely difficult to detect.

Because of the value the victim can bring to the attackers, attackers will spend considerable time and effort to construct an email that looks as authentic as possible. Attackers will additionally research the intended victims via Facebook, Twitter and LinkedIn pages to get more personal details to add to their attack. Because of the sophistication and success of these type of attacks, we see a dramatic increase in their frequency.

What Employees Should Look Out for to Protect Your Business

Now that we have covered what phishing is and the risks involved, the remaining question is, how do you protect your business? Honestly, the methods that you and your employees need to implement do not require much more than paying attention to certain important details. Here are six tips and tricks to think about when you receive an email. These simple steps may prevent you and your employees from falling victim to a phishing attack.

1. When reading your emails, slow down. Frequently, spammers will create a sense of urgency in the messages they send. This tactic is designed to cause stress with the hope that you will overlook the minor details. When you receive a message like this, be careful to review the message. When in doubt, if you know the sender, make a phone call to confirm the message is real.

2. Investigate the facts. If you're receiving an unsolicited email, text message or phone call from a company, take the time to do some research. Often, they will include a phone number to call. Google the phone number to see if it is listed as a real phone number for that company. If you find the same phone number coming up as suspected Spam, you know your intuition was right.

3. Confirm where the link takes you. Using your mouse, hover over the links in an email (do NOT click, just hover) and verify that the link address will take you to where it says they will. For example, if the email says it is from Wells Fargo Bank, make sure any links in the email take you to the Wells Fargo website by hovering your mouse over the link. The link should clearly point to "wellsfargo" in some capacity. Make sure it does not go to any subdomain that looks similar to wellsfargo, such as connect.wellsfargo.bank.com. That is not a legitimate link.

4. Be wary of downloads. If you don't know the sender of the email or you are not expecting an email with an attachment, be cautious. If you are able, call the sender and confirm with them that they sent the email in question.

5. Your long-lost relatives are fake. If you receive an email claiming to be or to know of a long lost relative, delete the email and move on. Those type of emails is almost guaranteed to be fake.

6. Look out for your boss. If you receive an email from your boss asking that you do something unusual and to not ask any questions, sound the alarm. Double check with a phone call before moving forward. You cannot be too careful.

Cyber-security tools your business can implement

Now that we have covered methods to use to identify malicious email, let's look at a way to keep the emails out of your employees' inboxes in the first place. Here are seven security tools your business should consider using to help protect your employees and your company data.

1. Spam filtering. Make sure you have a spam filtering system in place that uses the latest technology, such as Artificial Intelligence, to reduce the number of malicious emails that get through.

2. Firewalls. Your company should implement a Next-Generation firewall that has advanced security features such as Geo-IP blocking. This helps to prevent your users from connecting to sites hosted in foreign countries that are known to steal or send malicious data.

3. Implement Next-Generation Anti-virus technologies such as End-Point Detection and Response tools on your servers and end-user computers. Ensure that you are using the latest technology to protect your workstations and servers. Artificial intelligence is an important ingredient. You will need to arrange this through an IT professional as the best technology is not typically sold directly to consumers and can only be installed by a professional.

4. Make sure your company implements Multi-Factor Authentication. Multi-Factor Authentication helps protect logins to sensitive applications by requiring users to have two things: something they know, such as a password and username, AND something they have, such as a smartphone or cryptographic token. When Multi-Factor Authentication is implemented, even if a password is compromised using a technique like spear-phishing, it's of no use to an attacker without the physical device held by the real end-user.

5. Implement strong and long passwords. It is not enough to have a strong password anymore. The length of the password plays a big part in security. I recommend that your company password policy call for passwords that are at least 14 charters long and complex.

6. Educate your employees. Companies should increase awareness of malicious emails and tactics by actively training employees and highlighting spear-phishing attacks as an important threat. Training programs often include "fake" emails that test users on their ability to identify fake and malicious emails. Systems like these help employers identify who needs training and what type of training would be the most effective.

7. Outsource your security. Security is ever-changing, and it takes a team to stay on top

of it. It is best that you outsource your security to a team that has the tools and experience to protect your business. It is what they do all day, every day and it is their job to do everything in their power to keep your business safe.

As a business owner, knowing how to protect your employees and your business can be overwhelming. Where to start is typically the first challenge. Like taxes or dealing with the IRS, cyber-security is not something you should try to tackle on your own. Look for an expert that has the experience, expertise and knowledge to understand the unique needs of your business. If you have questions about cyber-security or how to protect your business, contact the Network Builders IT team by following this link https://nbit.com/help-protect-my-business. Network Builders IT can assess what risks you currently have and devise a plan to best protect your business.

About the Author

Bill Bunnell is the Founder and CEO of Network Builders IT Inc., a Managed IT Services company and Founder and CEO of Cyberr Inc., a Managed Security Services Provider. Mr. Bunnell has over 20 years of experience in the IT industry. For the majority of those years, Mr. Bunnell has worked as a consultant providing network support for clients. Clients ranging from small to medium sized businesses to city governments, and publicly traded companies. Bill's roles have included project and technical lead for domestic and international mergers, global Microsoft Exchange design and implementations, and data center virtualization.

As CEO of Network Builders IT, Mr. Bunnell has built an award-winning IT company. Network Builders IT, IT has been named as one of the top 501 Managed Service Providers in the world in 2019 and 2015. In 2019 Network Builders IT was named to the Inc. 5000 list as one of the fastest-growing companies in America. Also, Network Builders IT, has won several industry awards from CRN and The Channel Company including the following awards, Tech Elite 250 and Next Gen 250 in 2018 and Next Gen 250 in 2017.

Network Builders IT is focused on providing the best IT services and practices while using the best technologies. Mr. Bunnell founded Network Builders IT with the specific goal to bring flat-rate managed IT services to the local market. Having been successful with that goal, Mr. Bunnell is now focused on providing Managed cyber-security services through Cyberr Inc., and better protecting business. As today's security landscape changes dramatically, it becomes increasingly complex and costly to protect a business.

If you have questions about Cyber-security or Managed IT Services, Mr. Bunnell is available to speak with you. Go to https://nbit.com/help-protect-my-business, to set up a time to discuss your questions and needs.

How to Develop a Business Continuity Plan

By Duleep Pillai

Disruption to a business can be costly. Lost revenue, as well as recovery expenses can be overwhelming. In July 2019, several areas of California experienced earthquakes, but, luckily, there was no major damage. However, what happens if your building collapses? Or a technological setback like cyber terrorism or hacking occurs? Do you have a plan for securing the continuity of your operations?

More than 60% of small- and medium-sized businesses do not have a way to recover from such occurrences. A Business Continuity Plan (BCP) serves to facilitate a fast, efficient and tested process for getting back on track with the least possible downtime. It also instructs all employees on what to do and what should happen.

What is a Business Continuity Plan?

A Business Continuity Plan (BCP) is a system of prevention and recovery against potential threats to that company. Although a BCP is often mistaken for a Backup and Disaster Recovery (BDR) plan, there is a marked difference. A BDR focuses mainly on the restoration of an IT infrastructure and its operations, whereas a BCP's focus is on the company as a whole, including IT infrastructure. A BCP helps ensure the protection of company's assets and personnel in the event of unforeseen disruptions from both natural disasters and human intervention.

Why do you need a Business Continuity Plan?

A BCP can be implemented in any business—large or small—but let's look at a single-owner business. What would happen to a business, its employees and customers if something happens to the owner? The "Bus Factor" may come into play here. The "Bus Factor" is a measurement of risk from information or capabilities that reside with only one key person. If that person were hypothetically "hit by a bus", would the company have the capability to function?

Advantages:

Businesses with a BCP in place can address this, and in a competitive market, provide a number of advantages over those that do not have one.

- Customer Confidence: Customers and prospects will trust a company with a BCP. In the case of a small business, customers have confidence that even in a disaster, the company has a plan to recover and continue as per normal operations.

- Employee Morale: A BCP provides assurance to employees that their jobs will be secure. A BCP demonstrates that employees are valued, in turn motivating them to be productive and loyal. It is important to also involve employees in the planning and testing phases so they will know exactly what will happen in a disaster.

- Vendor Relations: Vendors will trust a company with a BCP. They might be more willing to extend credit and other incentives if they know that their partner is prepared for unexpected situations.

- Better Efficiency: A business with a tested BCP will know how to respond efficiently to unforeseen circumstances, minimizing financial losses and costs. Many insurance providers now ask if their clients have a BCP in place.

Steps to Building a Business Continuity Plan

Step 1: Determine all potential risks that could affect your company.

Companies often have to assign a specific team for this task. Some of the potential threats may be easy to identify and some may require more re-search to identify.

Step 2: Complete a Business Impact Analysis to determine how the identified risks will affect operations.

Following this, your company will have to develop plans, safeguards, and procedures for recovery from the aforementioned risks. This is an extremely important step to ensure systems are recovered and employees know how to resume tasks.

Step 3: Test your BCP.

Without testing, it is impossible to know whether your plan is effective and if your company will be well-prepared to deal with major setbacks. A prop-er test utilizes one of the most serious disaster scenarios, one that would require the most involved and challenging recovery. Rigorous testing will let you know whether your plan is complete and ready for use or requires adjustments and retesting.

Experts often advise that a company practice their BCP with a scenario difficult enough that it tests the BCP's breaking point. Organizations typically test their BCP two to four times annually.

Step 4: Continue to review and improve your BCP.

After you have developed your plan, it is crucial that you do not let your BCP sit and become obsolete—continue to review and improve it so it remains relevant. Technology and employees are constantly changing and it's extremely important that the BCP evolves with your company. BCPs require the full support of an entire company, from upper management to junior employees.

A Top Priority

A Business Continuity Plan is one of the most important things to which a company should devote time and resources. When affected by a major circumstance—natural or technological—a BCP is the roadmap for moving forward. Therefore, the development of a BCP should be delegated to managers or those employees who are well-invested in the company.

Basic Building Blocks of a BCP

No matter the size of your business, BCP has the same basic building blocks. They are:

1. A Business Impact Analysis (BIA): A BIA is a multi-step report that outlines how certain events can affect the functionality of your business. A questionnaire should be distributed to all managers so they can identify potential risks and what consequences these would have on your company's functions and day-to-day operations. This analysis is often divided into two parts: a). inventory and b). risk analysis.

a. Inventory is the very first phase of creating a Business Impact Analysis and Business Continuity Plan. At this phase, information is collected about every facet of your company, focusing on its assets. It's important to dedicate a lot of time for this phase; collecting this information helps your company figure out potential threats to its functionality.

b. Risk analysis uses the information collected in the inventory phase and uses it to rank all your company's assets. Determine how to prioritize your assets and rank them in importance to your daily operations. It is also very important to define the Recovery Time Objective (RTO) and Recovery Point Objective (RPO).

Recovery Time Objective (RTO): RTO refers to the time it takes for a business to return to a fully functioning state. Depending on the type of business, the RTO could be days or minutes. For example, a business who can process credit cards in addition to cash or checks will have a shorter RTO verses a company who accepts only the latter two options.

Recovery Point Objective (RPO): RPO refers to the amount of disrupted time that can pass in relation to acceptable functioning. In other words, RPO is the threshold of productivity loss that a business can afford. If the business is using technology, the goal is to keep productivity loss to a minimum.

2. Functions and Processes: Next, document your company's functions and processes in order to assess how they could be affected by a disruption. This is similar to the information collected on the company's assets but focusses on day-to day-functioning.

3. Develop a Team: Put together a competent and qualified team to develop the Business Continuity Plan. They will need to identify all potential risks to your company, how these risks will affect operations, and generate realistic plans to put the company back on track as soon as possible.

4. Employee Training: Once the BCP is formed, it is crucial to train every employee regarding their role in the plan. If employees are unaware of what they need to do, the BCP will not work to its intended capacity.

Taking measures to keep the RTO and RPO values to a minimum can increase the cost of operations. However, these costs may be necessary in order to meet compliance requirements or maintain competitive in the marketplace.

About the Author

Duleep Pillai is the president of Veltec Networks based in San Jose CA. Established in 2007, Veltec Networks provide technology management solutions to businesses in Silicon Valley.

A seasoned IT and Networking professional, Duleep has more than 25 years of experience in the industry providing technology services. A firm believer in educating clients about how to secure their data and avoid pitfalls in the internet, he regularly speaks at events.

Holder of two patents, Duleep partners with other like-minded professionals to make Internet a better place for his clients.

Schedule an appointment with Duleep Pillai: https://duleeppillai.as.me

Veltec Networks, Inc
www.veltecnetworks.com
T : 1-855-5-VELTEC | 1-408-849-4441 Ext: 101

If you are interested in a Business Continuity Plan template for your business, you can download a free Word document here:
bcptemplate.veltecnetworks.com

The Importance of Email Security

By Jess Coburn

It was late on a Saturday evening and Officer Willard McNulty, nearing the end of his 12-hour shift, was finishing up his paperwork and looking forward to heading home to see his family. Just as he was wrapping things up, he decided to clear out his email before going off duty. He noticed a message from his department's "IT Administrator," warning that his password had been compromised and he was instructed to log in and change it immediately. McNulty, a good officer with an impeccable work ethic, clicked the link in the email and suddenly, the unthinkable happened. McNulty's computer screen locked up and like cascading dominos, the other systems throughout the government network followed suit. The police department, the fire department, the 911 call center, the water utilities, even the voicemail and phone systems all shut down, one by one. The IT team was called in only to realize an absolute nightmare was in progress. The entire computer network for the city had been infected with Ransomware and the hackers were now demanding hundreds of thousands of dollars in payment or they threatened to erase all of the city's data.

While this fictional story above sounds farfetched, for many cities it's all too real. At least 50 local governments within the United States have fallen victim to ransomware attacks recently, with the City of Riviera Beach being among the most recent. Their attack all started with a simple email; weeks later the city still hadn't recovered.

In 1999, I started my company Applied Innovations (www.appliedi.net) with the goal of delivering enterprise class Internet services to small and medium sized businesses. Today we're focused on delivering consulting services around security, performance, and innovation with the sole mission of helping businesses leverage technology to drive success. We help organizations secure their network, increase the productivity of their employees, and leverage new and innovative technology in a way that drives success for these businesses. I've had the privilege to help thousands of businesses, kept thousands of servers secure and online in the cloud, hosted hundreds of thousands of email domains, and managed millions of email inboxes. While no one can deny the Internet has revolutionized our time, email has been the catalyst that's fueled that change.

In our early days at Applied Innovations, our core offering was managed web hosting and email was a bonus feature. Providing email services was inexpensive and a 'nice to have' feature. Businesses quickly caught on to how email could change the way they operated and before long email went from a 'nice to have' to mission critical. Today there are more than 3.9 million active email users globally that send 293 billion emails every day.[12] Email hasn't just changed modern business; it's changed the business of crime as well.

Email Has Changed Business, The Business of Crime

Verizon recently announced that 94% of all detected malware was delivered via email. Symantec found that the threat of an email-based attack spans across all industries. Manufacturing alone has more than 98% of all malware attacks being email-borne.[13] It's not only malicious attachments and malware we need to worry about though. Hackers are leveraging phishing and impersonation to compromise business email accounts. Business email account compromise – where a hacker gains access to your or your employees' email messages – means big business for hackers. The median cost of a Business Email Compromise according to the FBI's Internet Crime Complaint Center is $24,439 or roughly the average price of a

---

[12] Group, R. (n.d.). Retrieved from https://www.radicati.com/wp/wp-content/uploads/2017/12/Email-Statistics-Report-2018-2022-Executive-Summary.pdf
[13] https://www.symantec.com/content/dam/symantec/docs/reports/istr-24-2019-en.pdf

used car in America.[14] Once an attacker gains access to your email account, they've gained access to all of your messages including shared documents and secrets. It doesn't stop there, though; they can even reset your online passwords and send emails from your account masquerading as you. They may send an email requesting human resources to change your payroll direct deposit account. They may mass email your contacts with a document that turns out to be ransomware. They might even request your employees to purchase gift cards, make wire transfers or buy plane tickets all while masquerading as you.

According to the Dark Web Market Index, your entire online identity could be purchased for around $1200 today.[15] Your bank account credentials sell for $259, your driver's license goes for $27, your Amazon accounts for $30 and even your Fortnite account is worth just over $11. The fact is what's in your email is extremely valuable, extremely targeted, and remarkably at risk.

---

[14] Verizon. (n.d.). Retrieved from https://enterprise.verizon.com/resources/reports/2019-data-breach-investigations-report.pdf
[15] DWBINdex. (n.d.). Retrieved from https://www.top10vpn.com/news/privacydark-web-market-price-index-2019-us-edition/

How Business Email Account Compromises Are Being Carried Out

Today's cybercriminals are predominantly using two different classes of attack against email: malware delivery and phishing.

Malware and the threat that lurks within the click

Malware delivery is straightforward. The hacker will send you an email with an attachment. This attachment could appear to be a simple invoice, proposal or spreadsheet. It takes a single click to open the wrong attachment and compromise your systems. Microsoft Office attachments represent 48% of all malicious attachments[16] and carry devastating payloads.

Today there are five types of Malware attacks or payloads that we need to protect our businesses' email against:

Viruses

A computer virus is a snippet of malicious code that's inserted into an otherwise innocuous application. When executed, the virus corrupts your computer files. This type of attack became well known throughout the '80s and '90s when users

---

[16] https://www.symantec.com/content/dam/symantec/docs/reports/istr-24-2019-en.pdf

would share programs and data using portable devices like floppy disks.

Worms

Worms are similar to viruses in how they affect computers except that they can replicate themselves and spread across networks. Worms are very dangerous and still commonly used as part of cyberattacks as they're able to replicate themselves very quickly via email.

Trojans

Trojans create a backdoor into your computer that allows hackers to take control of your computer without your knowledge. Trojans have been used to launch massive distributed denial of service attacks, and to steal personal information from your computers and computer networks. Personal data, like social security numbers, bank account details, website usernames, and passwords are all at risk. The Zeus trojan for example, was originally identified in 2007 and in 2010 the FBI arrested a team of hackers responsible for the trojan and noted that it and its variants were used to steal more than 70 million dollars.[17]

Spyware

Spyware is a type of malware that monitors the actions of the victim and reports back this information to hackers. A lot of spyware is used in phishing attacks to gain knowledge to perform

[17] Zeus, W. (n.d.). Retrieved from https://en.wikipedia.org/wiki/Zeus_(malware)

more targeted and lethal attacks. Browser extensions, Toolbars, and tray apps are all examples of possible spyware. Imagine if the 'birthday reminder, quote of the day or coupon app' was stealing all of your bank credentials and allowing hackers to empty your savings?

Ransomware

Ransomware is malware that encrypts your computer files. It then holds your data hostage until you pay a fee for the decryption key. Ransomware can spread like a worm across your network. Ransomware also frequently includes a trojan so that the hacker can enter your network through the back door and further exploit your systems before carrying out his attack. Ransomware can lay dormant for months before initiating an attack. Some Ransomware will even go as far as to disable antivirus software and backup software so that once the attack is underway, you have no choice but to pay the ransom. Ransomware attacks have dominated the headlines. As mentioned, in 2019 the city of Riviera Beach was in the news as the city had decided to pay their attackers the $600,000 ransom demanded after they were attacked. The Riviera Beach attack hits home for me as it's also the city where I went to elementary and middle school. Ransomware is such big business that there's even Ransomware as a Service (RaaS). The developers of the GandCrab RaaS recently announced that they were closing shop and retiring as they had generated more than \$2 billion in extortion payments from victims in just 18 months.[18]

Phishing and are you who you say you are?

Phishing is where things start to get a bit more complicated as 1 in every 99 emails is a phishing email.[19] Phishing is a fraudulent attempt to get someone to disclose private information by impersonating another entity.

The most common families of phishing attacks we see today are:

Mass Phishing Attacks

The attacker casts a wide net and sends the same generic email to a massive number of targets in hopes of getting a few to click.

Spear-Phishing

Where phishing is casting a wide net to a massive number of targets, spear-phishing is a targeted attack at a single individual. These attacks are more dangerous because the attacker will take the time to hunt his prey. They study social profiles, company websites, and news releases and target their individual with the information they find.

---

[18] Security, K. o. (n.d.). Retrieved from https://krebsonsecurity.com/2019/07/whos-behind-the-gandcrab-ransomware/
[19] Avanan. (n.d.). Retrieved from https://www.avanan.com/global-phish-report

Whaling

Whaling is not very different from spear-phishing. Here the attackers are targeting high-value C level executives like the CEO, CFO or COO.

There's a wide range of phishing techniques utilized but what we see most exploited today include:

Email Impersonation

Email Impersonation is where an email is being sent with the name of a familiar individual but using a different email address. Let's assume your CEO is Bob Jones and Bob Jones is traveling this week. We know this because, like all CEO's, Bob is active on social media, including posting pictures on Facebook and he is very diligent about keeping his autoreply up to date. You receive an email from Bob that appears to have been sent hastily from his personal email account bobjones1942 @gmail.com. It reads:

"Joe, I'm jumping on a plane to head to my client meetings. I am meeting with our clients and meant to bring them some gifts. Can you expense 10 $100 Amazon gift cards for me from Walgreens on 5th and Main and send me the numbers and PINs from the back? Just reply to this email message so I don't lose it. Sorry to put you through this. –Bob".

It's innocent enough yet very common and very effective. Our attacker has probably been stalking Bob for months. Today he saw Bob's Facebook post at the airport with #MIAtoLAX. He sent Bob an email and Bob's autoreply stated that he was traveling to meet clients and would be out of the office until Wednesday. With Google maps he found the Walgreens right around the corner from his office. He searched on LinkedIn to see who reports to Bob. Then, he created an online email account using Bob's name. Finally, he sent you the email, and you replied because you're a good employee and *BOOM* you're out $1000.00, and hopefully Bob will reimburse you. #UGOTPHISHED

Clone Phishing

In this type of phishing, a previously sent email containing a malicious link or attachment is used to create a copy of that email. For example, you might receive an Office 365 notification verifying that you just logged in from Lagos, Nigeria. You panic, click the link, end up on what looks like the Office 365 login screen and enter your email and address and password. It doesn't work, refreshes a couple times automatically, you enter your credentials again and you're in. You just got compromised.

URL spoofing

URL spoofing impersonates a URL within a phishing email. They might use similar looking character combinations that can be easily misread.

For example, https://www.rnicrosoft.com and https://www.microsoft.com could be confused when glanced at on your smart phone. You might receive a password reset notice with a link in it like this: https://www.microsoft.com.logins.management/password.aspx?jcoburn%40appliedi.net%26password reset%26appliedi.net. You focus on the www.microsoft.com part, not realizing that the actual domain you're visiting is a subdomain off of the "logins.management" domain. (Yes, that domain exists; I own it).

These attacks have one goal: to get you to compromise your information, and usually that's your email account. In March 2019, Barracuda Networks surveyed their customers and found that 29 percent of organizations had their Office 365 accounts compromised and used to send more than 1.5 million malicious emails without their knowledge.[20] Phishing, Malware, and Email Account Compromise represent a significant threat to your business, but that threat can be minimized.

10 Ways to Improve Email Security for Your Business

As you can imagine, the cybersecurity landscape has changed significantly and continues to evolve each day. We help our clients take a holistic approach to their cybersecurity and this approach reaches beyond just the computers and network.

[20] Barracuda. (n.d.). Retrieved from https://blog.barracuda.com/2019/05/02/threat-spotlight-account-takeover/

This list just a snapshot of what we do to help our clients today.

Multifactor Authentication (MFA)

The number one method to protect your employees from having their email accounts compromised is MFA. In fact, in 2018, Microsoft announced that their studies showed MFA could reduce account compromise by 99.9%.[21] MFA is an additional authentication step that happens after you've logged in. MFA should be enabled all critical accounts and systems, including email.

End User Training and Simulated Phishing Attacks

The problems for the city of Riviera Beach all started because someone clicked a link in an email.[22] For our clients, we recommend ongoing cybersecurity training in the form of micro training lessons. They're entertaining, only a couple of minutes long and sent throughout the year. We also perform phishing simulations throughout the year using the same methods and attacks that hackers are using currently. We don't only educate employees; we validate they're following the training.

Dark Web and Leaked Credential Monitoring

---

[21] Microsoft. (n.d.). Retrieved from https://www.microsoft.com/security/blog/2018/10/02/ignite-2018-highlights-passwordless-sign-in-confidential-computing-new-threat-protection-and-more/

[22] CBSNews. (n.d.). Retrieved from https://www.cbsnews.com/news/riviera-beach-florida-ransomware-attack-city-council-pays-600000-to-hackers-who-seized-its-computer-system/

Large scale data breaches are the new norm. There are more than 446 million records exposed.[23] These records span everything from social security numbers and drivers' licenses to the usernames and passwords to email and online accounts. Monitoring your employees for compromised credentials protects your business from exposed credentials.

Advanced Email Security Filtering

Today's modern email security filtering options include features like attachment detonation and time of click sandboxing. Attachment detonation is where the email filter intercepts attachments, test them in a simulated environment and monitors their activity to ensure they aren't malware. Time of click sandboxing checks the links you click on in your email at the time you click on them. Further, we always recommend both inbound and outbound filtering to help reduce the impact of compromise.

Email DNS Settings

With so many email issues, one would think there's something the Internet would do. Well there are: SPF, DKIM, and DMARC. SPF, sender policy framework, is meant to ensure emails from a domain are from trusted sources and can't be spoofed. DKIM, Domain Keys Identified Mail, enables an encryption key and digital signature to con-

---

[23] ITRC. (n.d.). Retrieved from https://www.idtheftcenter.org/wp-content/uploads/2019/02/ITRC_2018-End-of-Year-Aftermath_FINAL_V2_combinedWEB.pdf

firm if an email is authentic or spoofed. DMARC, "Domain-based Message Authentication, Reporting, and Conformance", brings together all of this information and dictates what a mail server should do when a message passes or fails these tests. The problem is that these settings are optional, and not every mail server or domain is using them. One of your first steps should be to ensure your domain and mail servers use these features.

DNS Security & Filtering

DNS security is quite involved. Simplifying it, you should ensure your employees are using secure, trusted DNS servers at all times. You should also be filtering known malicious domains and compromised websites.

Endpoint Detection and Response

IBM recently found scripting was used in the majority of attacks, and among those, Powershell was the most common.[24] The problem? These attacks execute in memory, and there's no file to find a signature against, and thus your antivirus isn't useful in protecting you. Modern Endpoint Detection and Response tools use machine learning and artificial intelligence to help identify attacks and malware that don't have a signature already. Your business should replace outdated antivirus with next-generation endpoint protection.

---

[24] IBM. (n.d.). Retrieved from https://www.theregister.co.uk/2019/02/26/malware_ibm_powershell/

Disaster Recovery and Business Continuity Planning

Let's face it, your business relies heavily on technology and has several threats looming. Documented and tested plans for when disasters happen are critical and secure backups are a must.

Cyber Liability Insurance

Cyber insurance is valuable today and can help reduce the financial burden when an attack happens. The city of Riviera Beach had cyber insurance and it absorbed much of the financial burden.[25]

Don't Secure IT Alone

It doesn't matter if you have a full time IT admin on staff or rely on Joe in accounting who's smart with computers, you shouldn't do IT alone and you shouldn't do cybersecurity alone. The fact is having an external expert or team of experts to lean on not only expands the expertise and experience available to your business but provides a higher level of coverage. Afterall, you don't know what you don't know.

Plan for Failure and Assume Compromise

When protecting against cybersecurity threats, you must be right every single time. The hacker on the

---

[25] CBSnews. (n.d.). Retrieved from https://cbs12.com/news/cbs12-news-investigates/city-of-riviera-beach-hires-crisis-managers-after-ransomware-attack

other hand, just has to get lucky once. In the past, the goal was to try to prevent every attack and build systems to be protected against every type of failure. The reality is that today you can't prevent every attack. Instead, it's essential to plan for systems to fail and assume you're already compromised and build your systems with that mindset in place. By taking this approach you'll recover faster and contain cyberthreats much easier. It's time to take a modern approach to cybersecurity within your business and that starts with protecting yourself from email compromise.

About the Author

Jess Coburn is CEO and founder of Applied Innovations, a leading provider of Managed Cloud, IT and Cyber-security services that is focused on helping businesses leverage their technology to drive success. Since 1999, Jess's team at Applied Innovations has assisted thousands of companies around the globe to get the most out of their IT resources.

Applied Innovations was one of the first two providers in the world to collaborate with Microsoft and build an all Microsoft Cloud on Windows Server and remains an active Microsoft partner and contributor to multiple early adopter and futures councils around cloud technologies. Jess has earned multiple certifications over the course of his career and has had the honor to serve on several advisory boards, panels and been a featured guest in multiple keynotes because of his forward-thinking and innovative approach to leveraging cutting-edge cloud technologies.

You can contact Jess online at:

https://www.linkedin.com/in/jesscoburn
https://twitter.com/jesscoburn
https://facebook.com/jesscoburn
Find his personal blog at https://jesscoburn.com

To learn more about what you can do to protect your business and your employees from email compromise visit: https://www.appliedi.net/emailsecuritytips

Endpoint Detection and Response vs. Traditional Anti-Virus

By John Kistler

Imagine that you're on an airplane. You have a window seat, over the wing. The sun is out, and the only other the person in your row has the aisle seat. No one claims the middle seat, thank you, Lord! Everything is right in the world and you'll be home before you know it. Life is good!

As the flight gets underway, the person sitting behind you starts coughing, sneezing and blowing their nose every two minutes. Patient zero with the latest flu bug spreads their sickness to all the passengers in proximity.

This analogy is much like the circumstances for malware and viruses in your PC. Every day, your hard drive is subject to a constant barrage of attacks. Both old and new variants of viruses, malware and other suspicious programs arise, with weird names like Trojan.cloxer or Petya ransom-ware. Each more strange sounding than the next, they infect your computer and run programs, log keystrokes, open ports, or spread to other computers on the network. Their goal is simple: get in, grab the credentials, and use the access to get your money.

Enter Endpoint Detection and Response (EDR)

EDR is different than traditional anti-virus (AV), a step up, in other words. Whereas traditional AV would have an ever-growing list of bad actors, bad websites, or bad behaviors to watch for and then suspend or quarantine, EDR uses tools to recognize abnormal behaviour in a particular file, process or program, then stops it and reports it.

"Well, that's great and all, but why do I need that?" you ask. After all your AV has worked great for twenty years to protect your computer so why try something new that you don't really understand? The answer: Today's threats actually evade your old AV, and quite effectively.

Paths of Least Resistance

Email is currently the most prevalent attack vector, with various messages and subject lines designed to pique your curiosity. Hackers use exciting messages like, "You have a package!" or "Check this

Out!" Warning messages like "Your account will expire soon" or "Your account is over quota" are also used to encourage unsuspecting users to open them. These phishing schemes are designed to trick you and try to get you to click on the link presented.

Closely behind email are infected websites that you visit while surfing the web. Webpages pop up and an alarm sounds, "Your hard drive is in Danger!" or "FBI Alert" or "Homeland Security". Maybe there's a phone number to call for salvation: "1-866-TROUBLE!" You're stuck, the virus is right in front of you, just waiting for a simple click. More people than you could imagine fall for these scams and call the number.

The third is an unpatched computer or zero-day exploit. It's like an open window into your house— very open, no screen, the bugs are just flying in, and there's no stopping them. Just five or so years ago, it was the operating system that needed patching every so often. Today, it's every program, and every browser as well as the operating system. That's a lot of patching and we can't do it often enough to keep up.

Yesterday vs. Today & Tomorrow

Let's compare the antivirus software of yesterday with the EDR of today and the future. In the past, AV programs used ID or heuristics to determine if a file should or shouldn't be allowed into your computer. Imagine all the files streaming in from the internet with a big bodyguard looking at their IDs as they try to enter, "Next, and next, and next and... gotcha!" A virus is identified and your AV program sends out an alert, asking you for instructions. Should we quarantine him or execute him? Most of us pick "quarantine." We look at the filename—because it's like a car accident on the other side of the highway. Of course, we have to look due to our natural curiosity. This process continues file by file, day by day, with the bad guy file list ever increasing.

Eventually, cyber criminals started something new – inventing spyware, trojans, worms, ransomware, fileless malware and hybrid attacks that mix and match into something truly hideous. These files breeze by traditional AV software because AV is only looking at each virus' ID and this new type of attack is hiding—the ID doesn't matter anymore. Plus, traditional AV can't scan your PowerShell, which automates your computer's operating system and tasks. Today's viruses can literally burrow into your PowerShell, logging all your keystrokes with a keylogger and sending all the information to the mothership. There, your activity is dissected and used to inform more advanced phishing attempts. Perhaps it's cryptocurrency they are after, all those bitcoins in your computer. You notice that the fan on your computer is louder than normal and commands are slower than normal—that's crypto-jacking running amok, using your CPU power, your graphics card and your electricity to mine your bitcoins and transfer them to someone else. These never stop until they get your money.

EDR recognizes all abnormal system activity, stops it and reports it. In doing this, EDR software works to dramatically drop the infection rate of a computer.

In essence, EDR is like a high-level security guard running around your computer constantly, one who never takes breaks. This employee is constantly checking various programs, processes and other commands, taking into account what is happening with each and every one. Sure, viruses get in because that's what viruses do. One particular virus— let's name him Viral Vinnie the Villain (Triple V)— thinks he's landed on a new uncharted planet. He happily grabs his virus flag and screams, "Eureka!" or, rather, "Vireka!" as he plants it firmly in your operating system. Now that he's in, he starts to add a nefarious process to an already-running system file.

Lo and behold, Sincere Super Susie (S3) sees this new activity and gets curious. "Hey Triple V! What are you doing?" she asks. S3 has been logging all the computer's activity, seeing Triple V the moment he walked in the door. She's monitored his every step, opened a case and proceeds to stop his movements, reporting him to central command. Central command has real-life staff, people who are serious about your computers' security. In real time, they report that Triple V tried to start a process that was recognized as virus-like or non-specific process-type behavior. Not only did S3 shut down V3's extra-curricular activity, S3 notified the real people at central command who in turn notified you. Your report is essentially a play-by-play of all V3's nefarious activities, as well as an explanation of how he was shut down, deleted, and stopped.

If you only have traditional AV, your computer is much more exposed; it's essentially junior league against major league. You need EDR to play as a professional, and to combat the next generation of viruses and malware. You need a team of experts who are monitoring your processes and making sure you are protected. You need an audit trail for when a virus does get through and you require protection from a breach or leaked data. Don't leave your business open to that kind of risk. Endpoint Detection and Response is the answer.

About the Author

John Kistler is the owner of J&B Technologies, Ltd., a technology-based IT firm in St. Louis Missouri since 1993.

From a modest start of just supplying computer components to individual users back in the early 90's, JBTech grew into a full network managed services technology firm, offering a wide range of services. Their concept of cradle to grave complete IT support for their clients' computer network includes helping plan and design IT infrastructure according to users' specific needs, helping implement and support the infrastructure after rollout and meeting the budget and time constraints as clients' businesses grow. From small businesses with just one desktop computer to large, complicated corporate networks complete with an in-house IT staff, JBTech helps everyone with all their daily technology needs. Within the last five years they've seen tremendous growth in complexity of the average computer network, along with the explosion of cybersecurity threats and government regulations to handle this new threat landscape. Their clients rely on them to help them navigate these and other issues and keep their networks secure and operational so that they can focus on their business.

Contact John David Kistler as follows:

Email: jkistler@jbtech.com

Ph: (314) 993-5528

www.jbtech.com

Securing Your Shadow IT

By Roy Richardson

According to a study by Gartner Inc., a global IT research and consulting firm, by 2020, 33% of cyber-related attacks will come from shadow IT sources. Gartner also reports that there are over 1,000 cloud services used by most large organizations and that 80% of end-users utilize software that is not vetted by their internal IT department. What this means is that shadow IT is inevitable in any business, so it is important that businesses understand how to secure the use of shadow IT and strengthen their IT system overall.

What is Shadow IT?

Shadow IT is any kind of technology-related activity or purchase of which the IT department is not aware. This can include hardware such as laptops, smartphones and tablets, software such as packaged and cloud services, and subscription-based "software as a service," or SaaS subscriptions. SaaS subscriptions are the most common security offenders because these tools are easily accessible to end-users and assist in boosting performance and productivity. Some of these applications may even be familiar to you: DropBox, Google's G Suite, and Amazon Web Services. Unfortunately, because so many of these applications are easy to access and seem benign, staff members tend to install and use them without informing their IT department or service provider. This can lead to some serious security threats, especially in highly regulated industries such as healthcare.

Bringing Shadow IT to Light

Without the oversight of an organization's IT department, there is no control over who has access to the application, whether the application meets the organization's security requirements, or if there are protections in place to prevent the risk of credential exposure. Lack of security oversight could ultimately lead to data breaches, lawsuits, or, at the extreme, the eventual closure of a business. Unfortunately, even CIO's grossly underestimate the number of cloud services used in their organizations by a factor of 15 to 22. In highly regulated industries, there can be up to 20 times more cloud applications running of which IT department is not aware.

There are three main security issues inherent in using shadow IT:

1. The first is difficulty in assessing and pinpointing which programs are/could be responsible for cyber-attacks or issues. If the IT department doesn't know how many and which applications are in use by employees, they have no starting point.

2. The second challenge for the IT department is the inability to manage risk due to a lack of visibility. How can they confidently assess the possible damage or financial liability to an organization that could result from unknown, unmonitored applications?

3. Lastly, due to lack of visibility and risk insight, it is rendered impossible to optimize and block malicious software or applications with security measures that haven't been created.

A Vicious Cycle

Oftentimes, an IT department's control over a business' technology may be too restrictive to employees, resulting in end-users seeking productivity tools and software not provided or approved by the IT department. This can lead to a disregard for IT policies, consequently introducing risks to a business' network and unbeknownst to the IT department. Typically, if the IT department can't see the risk, they won't know how to address it or prevent it from becoming a costly issue.

As helpful as shadow IT services are to end-users, the use of them without a vetted process, especially in regulated industries, can lead not only to serious data exposure but also heavy non-compliance fines. The costs don't end there, however. In health care, for example, if sensitive patient data stored in shadow IT cloud services are subjected to cyber-attacks, the business may be faced with legal damages for falling out of compliance. If an IT department loses control and visibility of data managed by users, they are unable to implement disaster recovery measures to mitigate these consequences.

Responding to Shadow IT

Since the practice of using shadow IT poses a security concern for businesses, how should they respond to its usage? Employees install software and applications they believe will enhance their work performance and productivity, so absolutely disallowing shadow IT may not be the most effective approach to alleviating issues.

An RSA study reported that 35% of employees needed to find loopholes in their company's security policies for access to tools that help them work better. What this implies is that the ultimate solution does not lie with further restriction of IT technologies. Rather, taking a strategic approach to understand the needs of end-users would help reduce the need for them to circumvent the process in the first place.

Communication, Training and Protocols

Communication and awareness are essential to ensure that both employees and network security needs are met. First, it is crucial that all levels of an organization receive cybersecurity awareness training to understand how shadow IT can negatively impact their company. In doing so, however, it is important to emphasize the organization's willingness to fulfill technology needs of end-users in such a way that will not pose a security risk. Furthermore, it is important to communicate and collaborate with all departments on the technologies they require on a day-to-day basis.

Some questions to consider include:

- What are the employees' IT needs?
- What don't employees like about their existing technologies?
- What kinds of tools would they like to see implemented?
- What is the reason for seeking additional technologies?

It is crucial to understand the challenges and pressures that certain departments may face and why they implemented the shadow IT resources they're using. From this informed standpoint, it becomes easier to create an IT infrastructure that is user-centric and responsive to the evolving needs of end-users. As well, the IT and security team are now able to investigate which apps introduce high risk, which of them are in compliance, how many users are using each app, and who are the top users of each app. They are then able to provide a list of approved applications that best fit the needs of both security and end-users. Lastly, investing in technology solutions that proactively monitor and block unsafe third-party applications in the network would prevent further vulnerabilities from infiltrating the business.

Setting Up a Business for Security Success

Ensuring that a solid framework is set in place regarding technology usage in the workplace will keep resources secure in the corporate environment. The model of "threats exist within and without" should be the foundation. In regulatory industries, this is especially important. Strict control is necessary to protect data and prevent unauthorized and malicious use of sensitive information. Luckily, there are platforms used by security experts (like ourselves at Aurora InfoTech) that provide the visibility, application risk insight, and optimization that help organizations overcome the challenges presented by cloud-usage and shadow IT. Monitoring technology use, adequate data backup and recovery, software updates and patching, as well as constant fixing of vulnerabilities are all crucial services.

Cybercriminals: A Profile

According to a report by the National Cybersecurity Alliance, 70% of cybercriminals deliberately target small businesses. They zero-in on these organizations because they tend to underspend on protection, they have untrained employees that pose a security risk, and subscribe to outdated practices for data protection. As a result, more than 60% of companies breached are forced to close their doors within six months. These businesses are the ones that Aurora InfoTech strives to support, and we do so especially with our managed IT security services.

The Necessity of Third-Party IT Services

You may be asking, "We have an IT department, why do we need a third party to manage applications and software, or even provide cloud solutions when we have our own?"

An external IT management service has the experience and in-depth knowledge of the security issues inherent in shadow IT that your department may not have. In addition, your internal department may not have been given the appropriate resources or training, or they are just too maxed out with existing responsibilities. Third party IT can work alongside internal departments as support, or provide additional oversight, monitoring and servicing.

About the Author

Roy Richardson is a co-founder, managing partner, and CTO of Aurora InfoTech LLC, a leading Cyber-security & IT consulting firm in Orlando, Florida. He started his first technology company over twenty years ago, providing remote IT support for small- to medium-sized businesses in the Dutch/French Caribbean. Over time, the company captured 65% market share for broadband and technology services. His executive management and engineering experience in cybersecurity, IT, and telecommunications allows him to relate to a broad spectrum of business and technology challenges. Roy believes in a proactive approach to cybersecurity and has the knowledge to apply strong network infrastructure and security practices.

About Aurora InfoTech

Aurora InfoTech is a cybersecurity firm that also provides Information Technology (IT) consulting, management, and support to businesses of all sizes. Aurora InfoTech believes in a holistic approach to cybersecurity, offering a range of services that include cybersecurity assessments, remote management and monitoring, data backup and disaster recovery, managed firewall and VPN, cloud-based business software, and network design. Offering also include security awareness training as well as quarterly business reviews and meetings to ensure all lines of communication remain open. Aurora InfoTech also offers support for internal IT departments.

Aurora InfoTech partners with industry-leading providers and in doing so, is able to utilize sophisticated, remote monitoring tools that auto-identify any existing or potential issues that allow for proactive service. Aurora InfoTech provides service with 24/7 security monitoring and management via its Security Operations Center (SOC) and Network Operations Center (NOC) with a 24/7 end-user Help Desk. With the evolving landscape of cyber threats, Aurora InfoTech aims to protect businesses and their continuity through strong network infrastructure and reliable security solutions. Aurora InfoTech strives to be a dynamic IT company where people enjoy working and clients feel safe.

Roy can be reached as follows:

Aurora InfoTech LLC

Phone: (407) 995-6766

Email: royrichardson@aurora-infotech.com

LinkedIn: www.linkedin.com/in/royajrichardson

Website: www.aurora-infotech.com

Book a 15-minute Hack Proof Strategy Session with Roy at https://calendly.com/royrichardson/ hack-proof-strategy-session

Insider Threats: What They Are and How to Prevent Them

By Michael Daley

Technology plays such a crucial role in our lives. People have personal gadgets, like smartphones and computers, that they use for work and vice-versa, work devices used for private purposes. Both realities pose a risk to the network and infrastructure that those devices are connected to. The data on these devices, whether sensitive or not, is always at risk.

No matter the size of your business, you need to be concerned about cybersecurity. The notion of "I'm too small of a target" is not applicable in today's growing world of cyber threats. You must be vigilant and trust your technology advisor on the ever-growing threat of hackers and cybercriminals.

In this chapter, we are going to discuss a common cyber threat in many organizations that most busi-

ness owners usually do not consider or plan to protect against — threats from the inside.

People are random, unexpected, and can change
their mind on something in less than a second. For
this reason, the technology that your company
possesses ought to be guarded against one of the
most significant cyber threats to your business,
your people! These folks include, but are not limited to, employees, contractors, subcontractors,
vendors, or anyone else that has some level of
clearance to access your data, network, and technology infrastructure.

Your own personnel, whether it be employees, contractors, subcontractors, or whoever else that you
employ to work in your company and have some
level of access to your systems data, is a risk to
those same systems and data they work with every
day. Whether it is malicious in intent or not, the
fact of the matter remains, we are all human, and
we are susceptible to mistakes. (For example, inad-
vertently downloading the latest cat video and not
realizing it is a virus in disguise!)

I cannot begin to stress how important it is to include insider threats in your overall cybersecurity
plan.

Facts to consider:

- According to the 2016 Cyber-security Intelligence Index from IBM, 60% of all cyberattacks were carried out by insiders. And of

those attacks, 75% were committed with malicious intent.

- The top 3 industries under attack are health care, manufacturing, and financial services.

- Personnel motivated by profit or grievance that steal or manipulate data are only a small part of the total danger

Some examples of insider threats include:

- Staff unintentionally sending sensitive files to the wrong person

- The loss of a flash drive with confidential information that contains sensitive information

- A disgruntled employee who leaves your company, but not before wiping out all of your data because that person had full administrative access.

- Employees who fall prey to phishing attacks and unknowingly give hackers their credentials.

So why should you be concerned? Well, it's your company's data and network after all. In the 21st century, I can guarantee the core functions of your business use technology to a certain extent. Whether your industry has compliance you must adhere to (such as HIPAA, SOC, NIST) or not, a cyber-attack could cripple your business. And unfortunately, it is happening to businesses every day!

Bring Your Own Device

BYOD is an acronym in the information technology world that stands for Bring Your Own Device. This policy refers to the permitting of employees' own technology into the workplace and using this to access and work on company resources. A small example of this includes sending and receiving company email on an employee's smartphone while a more significant example includes a laptop computer used to access sensitive information on a company server.

Ask yourself these questions: do you know what else is on your employee's devices? Does your managed service provider monitor these devices for security threats and the like? What happens if there is a breach and it originates from one of these devices? Are you prepared for this?

As a business owner, it is easy to trust your employees, especially those who have stood by your side for many years. But whether intentional or not, you must be cautious and prepare for the worst to happen. And that includes your most trusted employees going rogue and stealing or corrupting your systems and data.

Companies hire our firm to perform security audits, and after discussing the findings with the client, they instruct us to start the implementation phase of their new cybersecurity plan. We see everything from trusted employees who have been at the company for many years to brand new employees with full, unrestricted access to systems. When we reduce their level of access, they sometimes get upset and complain to the owner. They take it as no longer being trustworthy. As the owner, you must let your employees know it has nothing to do with trustworthiness, but it has everything to do with protecting the company, and ultimately your livelihood.

A Malicious Insider Threat Example

While there are hundreds of examples of breaches online (probably many more that do not go public, here is an example that was more personal as it was client of ours at the time, who instead of utilizing us to provide fully managed security services, entrusted their CTO (Chief Technology Officer) with the "keys to the kingdom".

After a few years in business, the C-level executives had some sort of internal conflict that was never fully disclosed to us. The CTO, who was an investor in the company as well, became disgruntled and, because he had all of the master credentials to their systems, he was able to (a) delete any trace emails in their own inbox that might have incriminated him, (b) lock us out of email administration, and (c) prevent developers from any access.

Luckily, we were eventually able to re-gain access to company email and remove this person's access, but this is still a lengthy and costly lesson learned for the company that went through this. With all of the proper security, procedures, and accountability in place before-hand this would have dramatically limited, if not eliminated, the time and expense spent to re-gain access and prevent them from regaining control.

An Accidental Insider Threat Example

There have been many examples in the news of breaches that have occurred because of threats from the inside. One significant case was the retail giant, Target[26]. In November 2013, a breach occurred which allowed attackers to gain access to personal information of customers including names, addresses, phone numbers, email addresses, credit card numbers, and other private data. So how did this happen? According to USA Today, "the state's investigation of the breach determined that cyber attackers gained access to Target's computer gateway server through credentials stolen from a third-party vendor in Nov. 2013." More specifically, attackers had sent an email containing malware to one of Target's refrigeration vendors, Fazio Mechanical, two months before the breach. Fazio, like several of Target's vendors, uses a centralized vendor portal. The attackers were able to access this portal via stolen credentials on Fazio's computer systems and thus, in turn, were able to

---

[26] https://www.usatoday.com/story/money/2017/05/23/target-pay-185m-2013-data-breach-affected-consumers/102063932/

breach their way further into Target's computer network. The final result? In total, this affected 41 million payment card accounts and the contact information of 60 million Target customers. An $18.5 million multi-state settlement was paid out by Target.

Protecting your company against insider threats

Establishing a "Technology Use Policy" for your company will help to set a standard for the use of hardware, software, data, and systems in your organization. When someone violates the rules, having a policy in place will help facilitate disciplinary action against them. You can't expect employees to abide by the rules if they don't know what they are.

You should always employ a policy of least, or minimal, privilege.[27] What this means is that users must be able to access only the information and resources that are necessary for their legitimate purpose. As an example, your bookkeeper may not need full administrative access to your accounting system as compared to your accountant, CFO, etc. That person should only need the permissions to be able to do their job effectively. This is not to say that your bookkeeper has bad intentions, BUT if their credentials get lost or stolen a hacker could

---

[27] https://en.wikipedia.org/wiki/Principle_of_least_privilege

access your entire financial system with unrestricted access.

Any form of access to your company's data ought to be logged, audited, and recorded. In the event of a breach, having this system in place will allow you to quickly see which person or account accessed or manipulated the data that caused the incident.

Ideally, have all of your systems logging to one central location if possible to see everything in a single pane of glass view.

Make it a requirement that all of your personnel go through a cybersecurity awareness training. This training, usually held online, teaches employees basic skills to help prevent hackers from getting into your network and stealing your data. Preventative measures such as not leaving passwords on sticky notes under the keyboard (if I had a nickel for every time I have seen this) where unauthorized individuals could use those credentials to access systems. The training most importantly helps change the mindset across your organization to a more cybersecurity forward-thinking.

Password Storage

Where do you store all of your credentials? Do not store your passwords in a plain text word document, sticky note under your keyboard/monitor, or in a notebook in a desk drawer. All of these places make it easy for someone to gain access to your credentials. There are many encrypted and password protected software solutions available today that allow you to store passwords securely.

Social Engineering

Social engineering is the art of manipulating people to give up confidential information.[28] An example is the manager at a retail clothing store. At the end of the day when she was closing, a call came in supposedly from IT support at the corporate office. They had her go through a series of processes on the cash register point of sale system and eventually requested that she purchase gift cards. This was a red flag and she quickly realized that this was a scam and reported the issue. This was an example of social engineering that could have gone a lot worse.

Your Incident Response Plan

An incident response plan is something I would strongly recommend crafting and refining, so you are more prepared for when a breach does occur. This is a documented strategy for when a breach does occur, and there is a transparent process on how to handle the reporting and remediation. If your company is under any sort of compliancy, then a plan like this is usually required to have on file.

---

[28] https://www.webroot.com/us/en/resources/tips-articles/what-is-social-engineering

Managed Security Service Provider

Lastly, I would strongly recommend bringing in a trusted technology partner such as an MSSP (Managed Security Service Provider) in your area to help plan out a robust cybersecurity policy. They will usually start by performing a thorough cybersecurity audit on your infrastructure and then provide recommendations on how to best protect your network and, ultimately, your business.

Five Strategies to Incorporate:

1. Employ a strict technology use policy (can be included in your employee handbook) that everyone must review and sign

2. Enroll employees in a security awareness training program

3. Employ the right security technology to protect your data

4. Audit all forms of access whether physical or virtual

5. Utilize a professional MSSP to help you to employ the best security practices at your organization.

HINT: All of these strategies should be ongoing and not just a one-time thing!

About the Author

Michael Daley is the owner of a Managed Security Service Provider called TECH2BIT, located in Dayton, Ohio. His company offers complete, managed technology solutions for business clients who range in size from 10 to 500 employees. His clients are focused on growing their business rather than their information technology department. That's where an MSSP comes in – to provide a fully managed technology support and planning team. Daley started the company in 2015, and it has been growing consistently year after year. The driving force behind this growth is the need for out-sourced technology support and strategic planning that only an MSSP can provide. They have the skillset and personnel to help your company make technology work for you.

While they traditionally handle all aspects of the technology of a client's business, they also have more substantial companies as clients that have a traditional in-house IT department TECH2BITworks with to provide cybersecurity, compliance, project planning, and other CIO-related services.

TECH2BIT
Centerville, OH
Ph: 937-477-0493

Please visit the following link for our FREE guide on how to protect your business against insider threats.
www.tech2bit.com/insider-threats

Backup Your Data Right, the First Time

By Igor Pinchevskiy

It's a beautiful Friday morning in Los Angeles. Bob, a partner in a 50-employee law firm, is at work. An email pops up in his inbox about an online order. He doesn't remember placing it, but decides to find out the details anyway. Strangely, the attachment that should contain the information is unopenable. It seems Bob's security features are blocking his attempt to open the attachment. Not one to give up, Bob decides to forward the email to everyone in his office, with the instruction to try opening the attachment then inform him of the contents. Maria, Bob's secretary, is able to successfully bypass the company's IT security through the personal laptop she brought to work. She opens the attachment, but it's empty.

Soon after, Bob's staff starts to complain that they are unable to open their files and applications. He calls their IT company about these issues. They quickly diagnose that his company has become infected with ransomware. However, they assure Bob that the company has nothing to worry about because they have backups. Bob is relieved—the law firm cannot operate if all their client cases, discoveries, depositions, reports, and accounting files aren't accessible. However, six hours later, Bob is notified by his IT company that they actually cannot restore his files. Bob is livid. The last successful back up was 14 months ago and did not include the new server that was installed six months ago. He's at a loss and doesn't know what to do.

The Importance of Data Security

Now, more than ever, businesses of all sizes—from one-person companies to multimillion-employee companies—rely on technology to run all aspects of their business. Specifically, they rely on their data to serve their staff, customers and partners, vendors, and in the case of nonprofit organizations, donors and volunteers.

The news is filled with countless stories of businesses and government agencies getting ransomware on their systems and data. Ransomware encrypts all servers, systems and data. Once this occurs, no one can access any of their resources or data. In one case, the Atlanta Police Department has lost years of their dashcam footage.[29] When the *Atlanta Journal-Constitution* asked Atlanta Police Chief Erika Shields about the lost footage, she re-

---

[29] https://www.ajc.com/news/local/atlanta-police-recovering-from-breach-years-dashcam-video-lost/dowuJGBMcW7PLOdK0UhgJJ/

sponded:, "I have been asking since day one, '... Do we have criminal investigatory files that have been compromised?' And I have been told, 'No.'"

But Shields continued to say that years of dashcam footage from before the March ransomware attack "is lost and cannot be recovered." She explained that the lost footage could compromise DUI cases if an officer's testimony isn't sufficient. It's unclear how many investigations might be affected.

Imagine the implications of this lost video footage and the impact it will have on the community. Many criminals might be set free and many may not be prosecuted due to the missing video footage.

This is not the only high-profile case of ransomware that has occurred. As a matter of fact, major ransomware cases pop up in the news at least once a week. Everything from city halls and hospitals to police and sheriff departments have been affected.

Is the Cloud safe?

"I don't need backups. All my data is in the cloud." Assumption is the mother of many mistakes when it comes to your data. If you store data in a cloud, is it 100% backed up and protected by your cloud providers? If you ever decide to relax with a glass of wine and read through your cloud provider's Terms of Service, you will find statements like these:

Google:

We don't make any commitments about the content within the Services. When permitted by law, Google, and Google's suppliers and distributors, will not be responsible for lost profits, revenues, or data, financial losses or indirect, special, consequential, exemplary, or punitive damages.[30]

Amazon:

4.11. As part of using Amazon EC2, you agree that your Amazon EC2 resources may be terminated or replaced due to failure, retirement or other AWS requirement(s). We have no liability whatsoever for any damages, liabilities, losses (including any corruption, deletion, or destruction or loss of data, applications or profits), or any other consequences resulting from the foregoing. THE USE OF AMAZON EC2 DOES NOT GRANT YOU, AND YOU HEREBY WAIVE, ANY RIGHT OF PHYSICAL ACCESS TO, OR PHYSICAL POSSESSION OF, ANY AWS SERVERS, EQUIPMENT, REAL OR PERSONAL PROPERTY, OR OTHER ASSETS.[31]

Microsoft:

b. We strive to keep the Services up and running; however, all online services suffer occasional disruptions and outages, and Microsoft is not liable for any disruption or loss you may suffer as a result. In the event of an outage, you may not be able to re-

[30] https://policies.google.com/terms?hl=en-US

[31] https://aws.amazon.com/service-terms/

trieve Your Content or Data that you've stored. We recommend that you regularly backup Your Content and Data that you store on the Services or store using Third-Party Apps and Services.[32]

In a nutshell, cloud providers tell the customer that their service is providing access to your data but will not be held responsible for any data loss. That is the customer's responsibility.

It's not only cyber-attacks you need to worry about

Sometime in your computer usage history, you will likely need to restore some data from your backups. Accidental deletion or a rogue employee can happen. Even natural disasters like hurricanes, floods, mudslides, fires, tornadoes, and earthquakes can disrupt IT systems. Freak accidents like a building fire or flood, or even theft are among the many scenarios that threaten data security. It's important to have a rock-solid backup system in place and have it tested on regular basis.

3-2-1 Backup: Multiple Back Ups Can Save Your Data

It is only a matter of time until your security layers start to degrade (configuration mistakes, discovered vulnerabilities, disgruntled employees, failed

---

[32] https://www.microsoft.com/en-us/servicesagreement

patches, rogue firmware). Your only lifeline in these situations will be your backups. That is right, *backups,* plural. Use a multilayered security approach and design your backup system with the 3-2-1 Backup Rule to help bulletproof against any disaster scenario.

The 3-2-1 Backup Rule:

Ensure you have <u>three</u> copies of your data on <u>two</u> different types of media, with at least <u>one</u> offsite copy. Here is the 3-2-1 Guide I created to supplement the 3-2-1 Backup Rule. This information will help you with your backup strategy:

Three Common Mistakes:

Putting All your Eggs in One Basket: A common misstep is storing your backup data on the same server as your production data. I see this method on a weekly basis. Backup data should never be stored on any internal or external drives connected to the production server. Many scenarios, such as hardware failures, ransomware, and viruses, will make the backups inaccessible or very difficult to restore.

Set It and Forget It: Technology has made tremendous improvements in reliability, compatibility, self-healing and automation over the years. However, if backups are not continuously monitored, it is only a matter of time before they fail. Implement alerts that are configured correctly and a monitoring system that will notify you of critical issues that may arise with a backup so that problems can be addressed right away.

Not Testing Your Backups: There are a lot of things that can go wrong with your backup data. If you never test your backups, you may not be able to recover your data or recover it in a timely manner.

Recommendations

Protect your Backup Data:

Local backup data must be segmented onto its own dedicated VLAN with restricted access.

Create a unique username and password for your storage – never use an existing username and password.

Never join the storage appliance and/or server to the domain.

Implement the 3-2-1 Backup Rule: Make sure you have at least 3 copies of your backup data in at least two physical locations, preferably with one offsite.

Pick the Right Solution: You need to be confident that your equipment will perform no matter what happens. Make sure you are not using outdated or used equipment to store your backup data. Check that your vendor or partner's Service-Level Agreement (SLA) includes 24/7 support.

Here's What You Must Do

Verification & Testing: Verify and test your back-ups on a regular basis. At least once a month, execute manual test restores of files and booting of backup images (boot from backup). This will limit the probability of your backups failing during a recovery. There are many automated backup solutions that provide programmed integrity checks, as well as file, image, and boot up verifications, however, even after those tests, some backups can only happen manually. Sometimes issues arise with the server or media to which you are trying to restore or sometimes it's something in the backup files; that is why performing monthly manual restores is recommended. Although it is a time- and resource-consuming task, the resulting peace of mind and confidence in your backups is priceless.

So, what happened with Bob, from the beginning of this chapter?

Since the company's original IT company couldn't help, Bob looked for a better provider. Luckily, he found us at IP Technologies. We advised him that without current and working backups, his only option for getting his data back was to pay the ransom in exchange for the decryption key. However, that isn't always the end of the story. Once a company is hit with ransomware, they may be vulnerable to sub attacks. The attackers have all the company's information and can attack again. Our company, IP Technologies, always recommends a full sanitization of the network and systems in order to prevent sub ransomware attacks on a network. This is what we recommended to Bob. When we came in, recovering the company's data took four days of complete downtime, costing the company $6,500 in ransom, about $23,000 in lost employee productivity and about $55,000 in lost revenue. All of this could have been avoided—and would have cost much less— if Bob had chosen an IT company that had specific expertise and experience in backups and data availability.

About the Author

Igor Pinchevskiy has been providing consultations to SMB (small and medium sized businesses) seeking help with their business objectives for over 20 years. Igor's expertise is in data security, disaster recovery, business continuity (BCP), and improving operational efficiencies. Igor has been serving his community by educating businesses on Backup and Disaster Recovery for Business Continuity, Cloud Computing, and Best Practices for Network Security which has proven invaluable to business owners and have saved numerous businesses.

Igor holds his degree in Network Engineering as well as numerous Cisco, Microsoft, and VMware certifications.

IP TECHNOLOGIES INC
Charlotte: 704-912-4999
Los Angeles: 818-486-9970

www.ingramcontent.com/pod-product-compliance
Lightning Source LLC
LaVergne TN
LVHW022320060326
832902LV00020B/3570